The Art of
HANDMADE
TILE

Complete Instructions for
Carving, Casting & Glazing

KRISTIN PECK

Published by

kp **krause publications**
since 1952
PO Box 5009 • Iola WI 54945-5009 • krausebooks.com

700 E. State St.
Iola, WI 54990-0001
Telephone 715-445-2214
www.krause.com

Please call or write for our free catalog of publications. Our toll-free number to place an order or obtain a free catalog is 800-258-0929 or please use our regular business telephone, 715-445-2214.

Library of Congress Catalog Number: 2002105087
ISBN: 0-87349-432-6

Printed in the United States of America

Photos by Joe Jacobs unless otherwise indicated.
Illustrations by David Peck.

Back cover photos: Clockwise—Michael Cohen, Bob Jewell, "Sun Tile,"
Linda Leighton, Diane Husson, "Les Cadeux de la Mer."

Dedication

This book is dedicated to my husband David, my boys, my mom, and to the memory of my father and Aunt Nancy. Thanks for your inspiration.

Acknowledgments

First and foremost, I would like to thank Krause Publications for the opportunity to write this book. I would also like to thank my editor Barbara Case and acquisition editor Julie Stephani for their support and encouragement. They made this project a lot of fun.

Many heartfelt thanks to the artists who contributed to this book. It was a privilege to work with them and have the opportunity to share their wonderful tile with others. Thanks to the experts who contributed to Chapter 10 for their insight and expertise. It will go a long way in helping others.

I would like to thank my photographer Joe Jacobs for his patience and help. I learned there is a lot more to taking a picture than pointing and shooting.

I am grateful to my husband David, whose illustration skills I took full advantage of.

Thanks to Mid-South Ceramics for their support and sponsorship. Thank you Tammy, Diane, and Bill.

I am deeply grateful to the people who spent their valuable time, sharing and supporting my dream of writing this book. Many, many thanks to Frank Giorgini, whose book put me on this path. Thanks to the people who contributed by taking the time and making the effort to answer any question I threw at them. Even before I decided to write a book, these individuals helped dig the pool of knowledge I now share with readers.

Thank you to:

Tammy Archer	Ruth Butler
Elaine Goulart	Diane Husson
Joe Koons	Erric Philman
Robert Swanson	Carol Taylor
Joe Taylor	Leeroy Warner
Nancy Weldon	Pam Wilson

I am grateful for the support of my family and friends, especially my friend Lisa Jett, who helped keep my feet on the ground.

Contents

Photo courtesy of the Moravian Pottery and Tile Works.

The Moravian Pottery and Tile Works.

Foreword

by Adam Zayas

Handmade tiles – the tiles made by using simple hand tools – exhibit a sense of humanity unlike any shown by the industrially-produced kind. The variety of color, surface, and texture is proof of the individual personality behind the tiles. They are more difficult to produce, more labor intensive, and in general require more attention than their machine-made counterparts. And yet there has been a dramatic increase in small producers throughout the country introducing new tile designs. The buying public has clamored for both new designs and ways to include these tiles throughout their residences and general environment. They look to give their homes soul through the use of materials and reflect the humanity behind their making as opposed to an overly refined machine aesthetic.

Founded in 1898 by Henry C. Mercer (1856-1930), the Moravian Pottery and Tile Works in Doylestown, Pennsylvania, continues to be a major producer of handmade tiles and also to exert a strong influence on the making of tiles by hand. Mercer established the pottery to pro-

mote the ideas of the American Arts and Crafts Movement, of which he was a major proponent. These ideas – of not using machinery, utilizing local materials, and referencing history as a design source – are still shared by many tile makers today. The thought was that by combining the unpurified local materials with hand forming methods executed by skilled workers, a unique product would result each time.

The first quarter of the 1900s was a remarkable era in terms of handmade tile. The incredible range and diversity of the tiles produced was in reaction to the Victorian industrial aesthetics of the time. The Moravian Pottery and Tile Works was one of the few tile businesses to survive the economic depression and war. Most tile makers were forced out of business, allowing industry to set the standard for tile until the latter part of the twentieth century, when a number of ceramic artists rediscovered tile as a form of expression.

Many of these new tile makers had come primarily out of university ceramic programs

Henry Mercer, "Cannibals," the Moravian Pottery and Tile Works.

Henry Mercer, "Destruction of Atlantis," the Moravian Pottery and Tile Works.

where making tile, if not looked down upon, was viewed as somewhat akin to ashtray production. Like Mercer in 1898, tile makers struggled to produce tile that could artistically rival those of the past. These new tile artists were able to come into the market with a fabulous array of work at a time when many architects, designers, and homeowners were looking for something other than the regular sameness that industry had to offer. As a result, we are now witnessing a renaissance in tile designing and making.

Tiles are being used in a great number of different applications, as they were early in the last century. They have become more popular in the northern part of the country in addition to their traditional use in warm climate areas. They are not just relegated to the bathroom but are used as decorative flooring, wall coverings, fireplace facades and hearths.

Tiles are made using any of a number of diverse skills and techniques. Many designs are modeled relief, others are carved, sculpted, inlaid with other clays, or painted. Some are a combination of the aforementioned techniques and others that I haven't even considered. Tiles are

not always square and vary in size from fine tesserae to huge tiles. Mosaic tiles are composed of a number of smaller tile segments set together to create a larger complete image. The variety of tile designs is astounding and appealing to both tile makers and consumers.

As head ceramist of the Moravian Pottery and Tile Works since 1986, I have had the opportunity to observe and play a part in the growth of the handmade tile field. In that time alone, the Moravian Pottery and Tile Works has had over a hundred apprentices who have come to us to learn the details of making tiles by hand. Our simple techniques, like those in this book, are readily accessible to both beginners and professionals alike. At the Moravian Tile Works we have made no attempt to produce uniform tiles. We believe that sort of rigid standardization to be the domain of machinery. Our goal has always been to make a tile reflective of the producer's touch and skill as well as the directness of the processes used. Many of our apprentices have developed their own businesses utilizing our techniques. I am pleased to find a number of our former apprentices among those featured in this book.

Introduction

Tile has endured for hundreds of years, leaving us with gifts from the past. Through the window of time, tile shares with us a rich history of life, death, and war. Because tile is so durable, it is a large part of our lives and takes many shapes and forms. Tile has become an intimate part of our existence, whether it is a simple white tile serving a purely utilitarian function or an intricate design to be enjoyed and admired. Walking into almost any home across America you will find tile of one type or another. While reading this book, you'll soon discover the unique contribution you can add to your home by filling it with handmade tile. You will also discover that the art of tile making will easily become more than a passing interest.

Imperfections are an important part of both the handmade tile process and the final result. This is very important to remember, because along the way in making handmade tile, you will find even your early attempts will have their own appeal because of the natural flaws of your learning period. You are not trying to create a perfect tile. The key to making a good handmade tile is to not try too hard. If you want perfect tile, go to the hardware store and buy it. At the same time, you are not trying to create "art." You are going to have fun creating something that reflects a bit of your own personality and style. After your tile is installed, it will endure, reflecting your own individuality. And it will be all the more valuable because of its imperfections.

Many people feel handmade tile has recently gained popularity for the same reasons it was popular a hundred years ago. Man is striving for technological superiority, which is reflected in our everyday lives. We are communicating through space, we are developing computers to make computers, and we are finding faster and more efficient ways to mass produce products. Which means everything is the same, everything is perfect, and frankly, everything is boring. So here we are with an artistic medium that can not only be transformed into tile of unique beauty, it can also be transformed into a product that for centuries has proven its value. While we are surrounded by technology, or more to the point, forced to live with it, we are not forced to live *in* it. People are spending more time at home, for both work and play, and still desire the human contact that is being phased out of our lives day by day. With tile, especially handmade tile, there is a human touch that is missing in today's products. Tile is an intimate part of our lives, greeting us every day throughout our home.

What will you learn from this book? First you will learn that there isn't a right or wrong way to do many of these techniques. I explain what has worked best for me, but as time goes on, you will discover what works best for you. As your interest in making handmade tile evolves, you will find that your quest for knowledge will go beyond this book. It will continue as it did for me, through books, trial and error, and people who share their knowledge and experiences. You will find that answers are only a question away. You may also find that something in this book doesn't work for you and you may find a better way of doing it. If so, my advice is to go for it but don't forget to share your triumphs with others.

This book covers basic techniques and touches on more advanced techniques you may want to try once you've mastered the basics. Always remember, your tile may not be perfect the first time around but it will still be beautiful and worth the effort. One thing is for sure, after reading this book you will make fewer errors than I did. I am well acquainted with trial and error and hopefully, through my experiences, I will guide you directly to success.

The best advice I ever received, which I'd like to impress on you before you begin, is to *document your work*. Unfortunately it took me a long time to accept this advice and make it part of my work process. If you don't write it down, it didn't happen (or you will not know *how* it happened). Keep a small notebook handy and write down all your successes and failures. The first time you can't remember how you did something, you'll see why I think this is so important.

After making thousands and thousands of tiles myself, I thought I knew most of what there was to know. I was wrong. Speaking with the artists featured in this book opened up new avenues of technique that I have yet to discover. The outpouring of support and the willingness to share has shown me that tile artists do what they do for the love of it. I hope that by reading this book you will find that making handmade tile is not only about making tile for your backsplash, it is about discovering something in yourself you didn't know existed.

Kristin Peck

Chapter 1

The
BASICS

Michael Cohen, four 6" x 6" blue stoneware tiles, hand stamped and highlighted with molten glass over the design.

Photo courtesy of Michael Cohen.

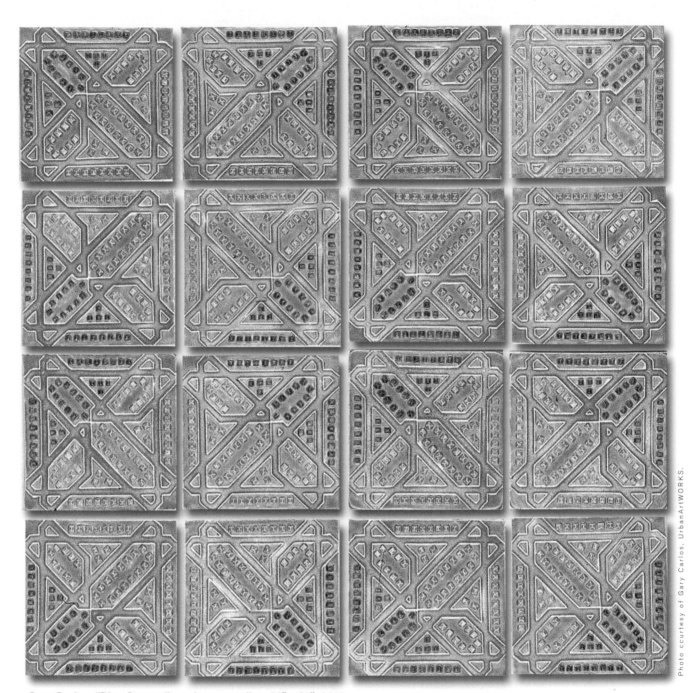

Gary Carlos, "Blue Streets," earthenware tiles, 23" x 23", 2000.

Karen Hailey, "Barn Scene," 2001, 4" x 4", white and brown stoneware.

Choosing the Right Clay

Clay – Hydrated silicate of aluminum. A plastic material that, upon firing, changes into a permanently hard waterproof material.

The main ingredient in the process of hand-made tile is the clay. If you're working with the right clay, the whole process seems quite easy. If, on the other hand, you've stumbled on the wrong clay, you'll ask yourself over and over why you ever started making tile.

I recommend that you purchase clay from a reputable ceramic supply house. I'm not saying you can't go out and dig up the healthy deposit of clay you have in your backyard. But keep in mind that you'll need to do extensive testing before using that clay for tile or any other pieces. Not to mention what it could do to your kiln. I've seen pots made of home-harvested clay melt in the kiln. For the sake of convenience and reliability, it's better to start with commercial clay.

Commercial clay usually lists its firing range, properties, best applications, and shrinkage rate. Commercial clay is inexpensive, consistent, and ready to use. It is sold in its moist state in increments of 25 lbs. An average 1/2" thick 4" by 4" tile weighs approximately 14 oz., so a 25 lb. bag of clay will yield 28 or so 4" by 4" tiles.

There are a few clays that make excellent tile and among those there is one constant – high amounts of grog and sand. This high grog content creates an open body, which allows the water between the clay particles to migrate to the surface. The open body helps the tile dry even and flat.

Earthenware – Earthenware clay is a porous clay body with a low firing range (below 2012°F/ 1100°C). Because of this low temperature range, you can take advantage of the huge spectrum of glaze colors available for low-temperature firing. Earthenware comes in an array of colors, which left unglazed make exceptionally beautiful tile. Earthenware will produce a less durable tile than stoneware, so function needs to be considered before it is installed.

Raku – Raku is also a low-fire body known for its ability to withstand the stresses of thermal shock. It usually has additions of fireclay and grog that help open up the clay body, giving it a coarse texture. Its firing range (glaze firing) is usually between 1652°F/900°C to 1832°F/1000°C. Some tile artists obtain great results with a raku body, but as with any clay, testing and firing within the listed temperature range is important to the success of your tile.

Stoneware – Stoneware is a dense clay with a good degree of plasticity that creates a strong and durable tile. It is usually considered a midrange fired clay, 2192°F/1200°C or higher. It comes in an array of colors, from off-white to red, and produces beautiful tile. Stoneware can be fired to vitrification, the stage where clay par-

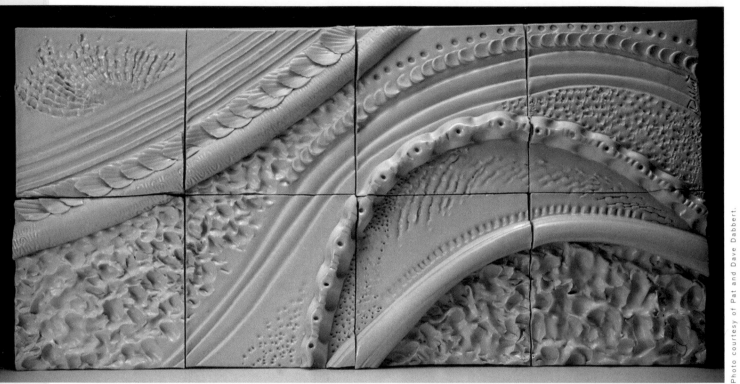

Pat and Dave Dabbert, "Ether Net," high-fire porcelain multi-tiled textured relief, glazed in soft semi-matt finish.

ticles are welded together, creating small porosity and low water absorption.

Porcelain – It is easy to be lured by the beauty and texture of porcelain. It has a smooth body that doesn't contain grog or sand. Porcelain is a high-fire clay that vitrifies completely, giving it a glasslike texture. However, porcelain is difficult to handle and even more difficult to keep flat. It takes longer to dry and the drying must be done with extreme care and patience or the piece will warp. You can put a perfectly flat bisque porcelain tile in a kiln for a glaze fire and watch it come out of the kiln warped. Unsurpassed in its purity, porcelain can be used for forming great works of art, but should be left to the advanced tile maker.

Look at clay as an entity with a personality. When you choose a clay body, you will learn its traits and its limits. At first, it may seem difficult to find an ideal clay, especially for tile making. Finding clay that is durable, warp resistant, and dependable is not impossible, but it does take a little time and patience.

I use and recommend white stoneware for a number of reasons. The first is its strength and durability, especially if it is fired to vitrification. Vitrified stoneware tile will have low water absorbency, which is optimal in a wet area. It is strong enough to withstand wear, and if you start off with strong clay, you won't have to switch clays according to its function. White clay will also give you clear bright colors. Experienced tile makers enjoy using different colored clays because they can anticipate their results based on experience. The beauty of red or brown clay is that it can be left bare to expose its natural warmth and richness. When you use a lighter colored clay body, you will usually get the color results shown on the glaze manufacturer's sample chip. White clay is also easier on your tile making equipment. Once your equipment has been used with red clay, it must be completely cleaned before you can use white clay. Red clay gets everywhere, so if your heart is set on using it, don't count on switching back and forth without serious cleaning.

It is not always necessary to fire a tile to its maturity (vitrification), but doing so will create a stronger tile. Always consider the glaze and the tile's intended function when firing. The durability requirements differ significantly for tile used for a floor, backsplash, fireplace surround, or shower wall. Tile installed in a wet area where it will be exposed to water should have a low percentage of absorption. The more porous the clay, the higher the water absorption. Clay that is fired to vitrification with a porosity of higher than 5% is

To prepare the scraps, stack the pieces and press each layer into the preceding layer.

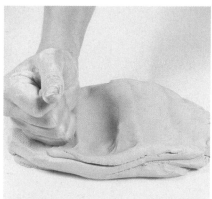

Pound the clay with your fist and fold it over into a compact roll.

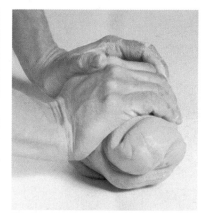

Wedge the clay with a kneading motion. You should be able to see a circular roll starting to form.

When the clay has become consistent and malleable, cut it with a wire to check for air bubbles. The clay can then be stored in its original bag or used immediately.

Reclaiming Tile Scraps

If your clay has been de-aired by the manufacturer, which it should state in the catalog, you can cut slabs directly from the block and make tile with the slabs.

During the tile making process, you will accumulate many scraps of clay, which you can reclaim for future use. Throwing the scraps back into the original bag is easy enough, especially if you intend to use the clay in the near future. If you don't intend to immediately use the clay, add a small amount of water and close the bag securely to keep it moist for another day. If the bag is closed tightly and there is sufficient water in the bag, the clay will stay moist indefinitely.

Reclaiming tile scraps is almost the same as reclaiming scraps for any ceramic project. It's very important to make sure the clay is clean and free of plaster.

considered earthenware. So although earthenware will make nice tile, it should not be used in areas that will be in contact with water or require strength and durability, such as a fireplace surround or a backsplash. Stoneware that is fired to 2192°F has less than 5% porosity, which means lower absorption, and is ideally suited to areas that require low water absorption and strength.

The firing range given for a clay body is just a guideline. If you are using a red clay body, keep in mind that if you fire at cone 5 in one firing and need consistent color, the next batch of tile must also be fired at cone 5. Although there are only

about 30° between cones, clay is very sensitive to temperature. I once fired a batch of red unglazed stoneware tile for a kitchen at cone 5 and installed it. The natural color of the clay was a beautiful deep red/brown. I fired the next batch a few days later but couldn't remember if it was at cone 5 or 6 so I fired at cone 6. The same clay came out a deep chocolate brown. Since the previous tile had already been installed, I had to do the whole batch over at cone 5. I couldn't believe 25° would have such a dramatic effect on the clay. Documenting my process would have saved me time, money, and labor.

A large electric kiln, which can produce hundreds of tiles with each firing and a small test kiln with a chamber that can accommodate two to three tiles at a time.

The Kiln

Kiln – Derived from the Latin culina, kitchen. A chamber where more heat is introduced than can escape, thereby raising the temperature in the chamber.

Scientists have found traces of kilns dating back thousands of years. Kiln remains have given modern man an insight into history's technology, art, and basic day-to-day living. The kiln is a wondrous tool whose basic principle has not been altered, only built upon, since its invention. The kiln fires the components of the earth into a glasslike material that is unaffected by water.

Wood-fired kilns are still used today and require the same amount of work and expertise that they did hundreds of years ago. A wood firing takes an immense amount of preparation, labor, and time. You must have the fuel – wood – chopped and ready to be fed into the kiln. A wood firing can take from hours to a week and must be monitored at all times. There isn't any

way to insure consistency with a wood firing, which is an important consideration when making tile. Fortunately, modern technology has stepped in to create kilns that are both easy to use and yield consistent results

There are two types of kilns readily available on the market – gas and electric. The gas kiln has a great deal of effect on both the clay body and the glaze being used. Specifically, it is the firing atmosphere that distinguishes an electric kiln from a gas kiln. Within the gas kiln there is a *reduction atmosphere*, which is achieved by taking oxygen away from the metal oxides. You can attain different colors from the same metal oxide in the clay or glaze, achieving a wide spectrum of startling effects. Many professional ceramists use gas kilns because of the character the firing atmosphere evokes on their work. A gas kiln is initially more expensive to purchase but because of its fuel source, in the long run it is much more efficient to fire than an electric kiln. A gas kiln will not fire itself, it must be monitored during the firing process. Besides the initial kiln costs, you will need a separate structure to house the kiln if you are firing at home and you will need to check local ordinances for permit requirements and have gas and power lines run to the kiln location.

The electric kiln, which is also readily available, is not only portable but also easy to use. The electric kiln has an *oxidation atmosphere*, where air is introduced through small holes or baffles, encouraging airflow within the chamber. The electric kiln is ideal for the tile maker. It will produce consistent tile from load to load.

There are specific issues to consider when purchasing an electric kiln. What size will you need? Do you need one with 10 cu. ft. or will a small kiln with $1/2$ cu. ft. work? If you are going to make a few tiles for yourself and friends, then a small kiln will allow you to fire small batches of tile quickly. If you intend to produce tile as a way to generate income, buying a large kiln will be a good investment. The more tiles you can fit in your kiln at one time, the cheaper it is to fire each piece.

Consider that if you are using a small kiln, sometimes referred to as a test kiln, certain glaze effects may be hard to achieve. Small kilns are fast firing and the turnaround time from heat up

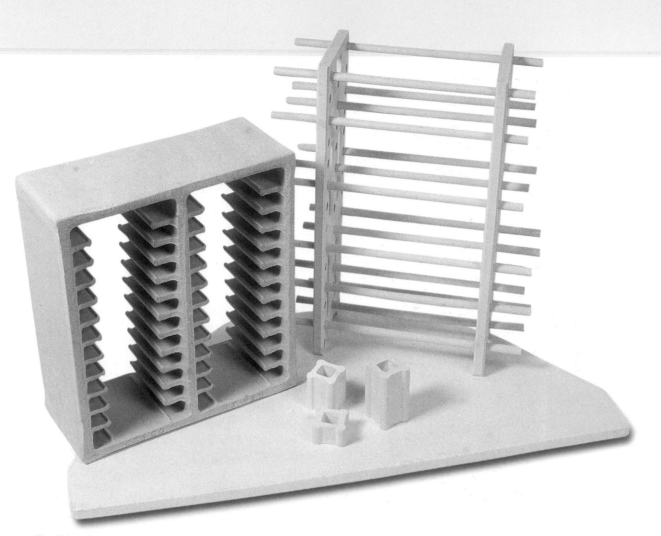

Traditional or specialized kiln furniture can accommodate tile. At left is a large tile sitter that can hold up to 24 4" x 4" tiles. At right is an open shelf system that can hold various sizes and shapes and up to 36 4" x 4" tiles. In front are square posts used to support the kiln shelves.

to cool down is impressively quick, but it is during the cooling phase that certain glazes such as a matt or satin are developed. If the cool down is too quick, your color will be true but you will have a gloss finish. With a computerized kiln, you can program it to slow down the cooling process. If your kiln is manual, you will have to keep all plug openings closed and allow it to cool down as slowly as possible. Smaller kilns are energy efficient and can usually be plugged right into a household socket. They are relatively inexpensive and can be used to fire numerous materials like metal, glass, and enamel.

If your kiln is a manual, it should have a cone sitter, a small mechanism that turns the kiln off when it has reached a specific temperature. Your kiln should also have a backup timer to insure that the kiln will turn off shortly after the approximate firing time if the cone sitter malfunctions.

Deciding on the maximum temperature or cone is easy enough. If you are firing a low-fire clay body, a kiln that will go up to cone 6 is more than adequate. If your clay body is midrange, you may want to go up to cone 8 or 10. Remember that firing at a higher temperature will wear out the kiln elements much faster than firing at lower temperatures.

If your budget allows, buy an automatic kiln. It will make your life much easier and the process less complicated. Today's automatic kilns schedule, delay, monitor, shut off, and ramp the firing. A good partner to the automatic kiln is a motorized vent, which allows you to completely close your kiln. The air is drawn in through holes at one end and pulled out through holes at the other end. A motorized kiln vent can be used with a manual kiln or a computerized kiln. With both kilns, a motorized vent will give you a more uniform kiln environment and a consistent firing temperature from top to bottom. Not only will the kiln atmosphere be cleaner, but also harmful gases that might seep into the kiln room can be directed out through ducting.

Common ceramic tools can be used to create tile. Left to right: small sponge, flexible rib, cutting wire, finger tool, wood modeling tool, wire end tool, potter's knife, flexible rib, stylus, wire/wood modeling tool, wood modeling tool, metal potter's needle.

Whatever type of kiln you use, always read the manufacturer's guidelines before you fire for the first time. You need to know what the electrical requirements will be, especially if your electric kiln will share a circuit in your home. Always place your kiln away from the living area, especially if you don't have a motorized kiln vent. If your kiln is placed in a garage, it's a good idea to cover the walls with fireproof fiberboard or a concrete board of some type. Read the guidelines and directions cover to cover when you purchase your kiln. And if you already have a kiln, it's a good idea to review the literature periodically.

If you are not ready to purchase a kiln, it is relatively easy to find one locally to fire your work. Joining a local ceramic club will not only allow you to meet other individuals with the same interest, but will give you access to other member's kilns. You can find kilns at city recreation centers, YMCAs, public schools, and small pottery outlets, which are popping up all over America.

Kiln Furniture

Kiln furniture is another important consideration when you buy a kiln. Kiln furniture is made of refractory material, a material able to withstand high temperatures without deformation. There are numerous tile sitters on the market, all with their pros and cons. Tile sitters are used to support the tile inside the kiln. The easiest way to load tile in a kiln is to place the tile on the kiln shelves that you can purchase as a furniture set with your kiln. The downside is that the space for tile placement on each shelf is limited.

Stacking kiln shelves with posts for airflow adds a tremendous amount of mass to your load and requires that you heat and cool the mass of each shelf. Using a thinner or lighter kiln shelf will not only help with the energy it takes to heat the kiln, but will allow the kiln to cool down more quickly. There are tile shelf units on the market that can hold as many as 24 4" by 4" tiles. These will work if you are making thin field tiles. The space between the shelves varies from sitter to sitter. A relief handmade tile will probably be thicker than the average tile and I find that most relief handmade tile will not fit within the shelf space. If you do succeed in squeezing them in and there is any movement in the clay during firing, the glazed tile will stick to the shelf prong above it. To get the tile loose, you'll need to use a hammer to break the shelf. Another type of tile sitter is an open shelf, which, although an investment, solves the problem of excess mass in your kiln. These allow you to stack the tiles

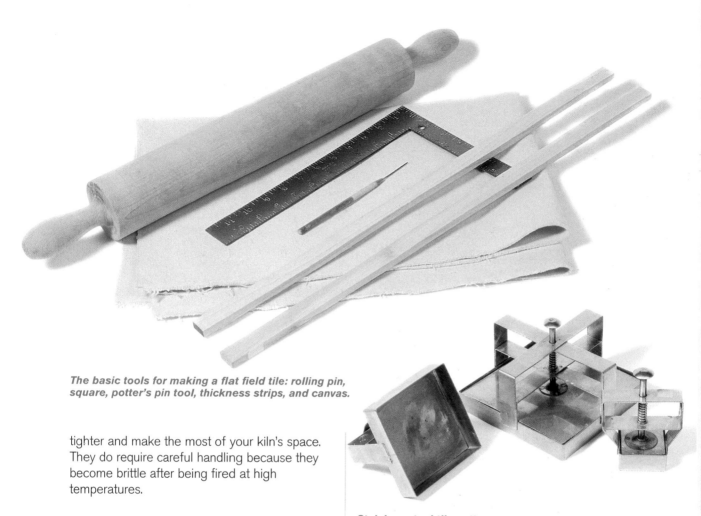

The basic tools for making a flat field tile: rolling pin, square, potter's pin tool, thickness strips, and canvas.

tighter and make the most of your kiln's space. They do require careful handling because they become brittle after being fired at high temperatures.

Stainless steel tile cutters.

Tools and Equipment

Tools

The tools for making a basic tile are simple items that can be purchased at a hardware store, arts and craft store, or ceramic supply house. Other tools and supplies are discussed with specific projects.

You don't need many specialized tools to create a basic tile but if you intend to make more than one or two tiles at a time, you might want to invest in an easier way to cut each piece. There are various tile cutters available on the market that range in quality and size. The tile cutters shown in the photo are made of stainless steel and are spring loaded. Although they are more expensive than other cutters I have seen on the market, they have been the cornerstones of my tile making and paid for themselves many times over.

You will need:

- **1 yd. canvas** - Used to keep the mallet from sticking to the clay during pressing.
- **rubber mallet** - Used to pound the clay into the plaster mold.
- **straight edge and square** - For cutting straight edges and square corners.
- **rolling pin** - To roll slabs of clay to the correct thickness for tile.
- **two $\frac{1}{2}$" x 24" strips of wood (thickness strips)** - One for each side of the rolling pin to ride on.
- **squeegee** - To smooth out the canvas markings.
- **cardboard** - To cushion the plaster mold.
- **potter's tool kit** - Basic tools along with a potter's pin tool and a finger tool for fine detail.

Slab roller packages, 24" and 30" wide.

A stainless steel manual extruder shown with accessory dies.

Equipment

Every ceramic catalog is packed full of equipment, which can be very expensive and complicated to use. While there isn't any process in this book that can't be done with the simplest of tools, there may come a time when you want to invest in equipment to produce higher quantities or just simplify the process. The following equipment will help the beginning tile maker. This equipment is not essential to make tile, and the list only reflects my opinion. Talk with other tile makers to get an idea of what equipment is best.

Slab Rollers

A slab roller is used to create consistent slabs of clay. They save time and energy, especially if you are making multiple tiles. Slab rollers range from 22" to 36" wide, with various table lengths. They can either be single or double rollers. Single rollers rely on Masonite shims to regulate the thickness of the slab. The thinner you want the slab, the more shims you add. Double rollers don't need shims, only a layer of canvas to protect the rollers from the clay. Because you are making tile, I recommend double rollers, not for the convenience, but because single rollers push the clay in one direction, while double rollers push it in two directions, which cuts down on uneven shrinkage and warping.

Manual Extruder

An extruder is a piece of equipment that extrudes soft clay through an opening, which in turn replicates that profile. In the past, extruders have been totally overlooked but recently wonderful books have been published that illuminate the diverse capabilities of extruders. An extruder can be used to create molding, trim, and border tiles. The body of the extruder should be stainless steel or aluminum, so it will not rust. Rust can stain your clay as it passes through, which will ruin the tile. The extruder handle should be long enough to allow for easy operation. Extruders are mounted on the wall, so you will need a wall with a stud so it can be securely fastened. Most extruders come with the necessary hardware.

Some manufacturers have taken notice of the surge of interest in tile making and have created dies specifically for that purpose. Most manufacturers sell blank dies, so you can create your own profiles.

Tile Press

A manual tile press allows you to produce tile at a much faster rate than hand pressing into a plaster mold. There are a few different manual tile presses available on the market. The one in the photo has a two-ton capability, which is adequate for pressing a tile up to 6" square. Getting a larger tile to press will be difficult, because you have a lot of area where your clay must spread out and fill in the detail. With practice, this press has the capability of doing one or two tiles a minute.

The molds are made of hydra stone, which is strong enough to withstand the pressure of the press. You cannot use plaster molds because they will crack on the first pressing. Hydra stone molds are basically made in the same manner as plaster molds and can withstand the pressure of a hand press. Hydra stone is available through most ceramic supply houses.

The mold is placed on the bottom platform and covered with plastic wrap. A pug of clay the approximate size of the tile is laid on top of the opening. A small piece of Masonite board slides into the brackets on the top platform and the lever is rotated pressing down. When the lever is turned to its original up position, the tile is attached upside down to the top board. The board slides out and the plastic wrap, which served as a release agent, is carefully pulled off. The board is then placed in the drying rack until it can easily be cut off.

While a tile press is an investment, it can be duplicated with a $60 bearing press with a top and a bottom plate welded on. Most tool or heavy hardware catalogs carry an array of bearing presses.

Ware Cart

A ware cart is where your tile will be during most of the production. Your tile will be on the ware cart during drying, on the way to the kiln for bisquing, and during the unloading. You can use the shelves for a staging area for glazing, and then back to the kiln for its final firing. While a ceramic ware cart is a big investment, a baker's

A manual tile press.

A ware cart.

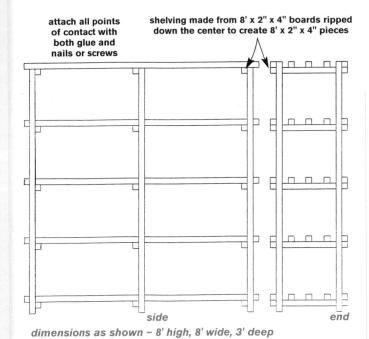

attach all points of contact with both glue and nails or screws

shelving made from 8' x 2" x 4" boards ripped down the center to create 8' x 2" x 4" pieces

side　　　*end*

dimensions as shown – 8' high, 8' wide, 3' deep

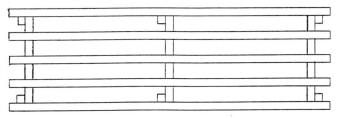

Drying Shelf

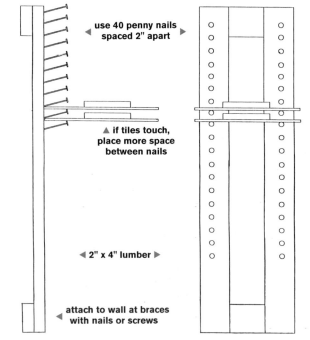

▲ **use 40 penny nails spaced 2" apart** ▶

▲ **if tiles touch, place more space between nails**

◀ **2" x 4" lumber** ▶

◀ **attach to wall at braces with nails or screws**

Pressed Tile Holding Rack

rack will only run you $50 or so. They are usually made of lightweight aluminum and are called cooling racks. You will have to make plywood shelves to slide in where baking pans are supposed to be, but they are very portable and can accommodate a lot of tile while taking up very little floor space.

Pug Mill

Pug mills are definitely an investment, but once you use one you will wonder how you ever did without one. A pug mill that not only pugs your clay but also de-airs it will cut down on clay waste. Every little scrap can be reclaimed and used again. Clay scraps are placed in the hopper at one end, and the de-aired mixed clay is extruded out the other end.

A pug mill that de-airs will have two motors, one for the pug mill and one for the vacuum that de-airs the clay. Make sure you get a pug mill that is compatible with your electrical service. A manufacturer should rate its operation by how many pounds of clay can be put through the machine in a given time. This is definitely a piece of equipment that should be researched before purchase.

Shelving

Shelves can be very expensive. The inexpensive metal shelving you see in department stores just doesn't cut it when you are storing pounds and pounds of clay for extended periods of time. Those shelves will warp and twist and are much better suited to the garage. After doing research on every shelf I could find, my husband ended up making ours out of 2" by 4"s. They actually look like Scandinavian furniture. Depending on where you purchase the lumber, a shelving unit should cost under $50.

If space for shelving is a concern, a drying shelf is an easy method for drying tile in very limited space. The tile will need to be placed on individual boards, but the rack can be as narrow as 12" and still hold up to 50 tiles.

Tile Display Board

Should you go further in tile making, you might want to document your work by applying sample tiles to tile boards for reference. The

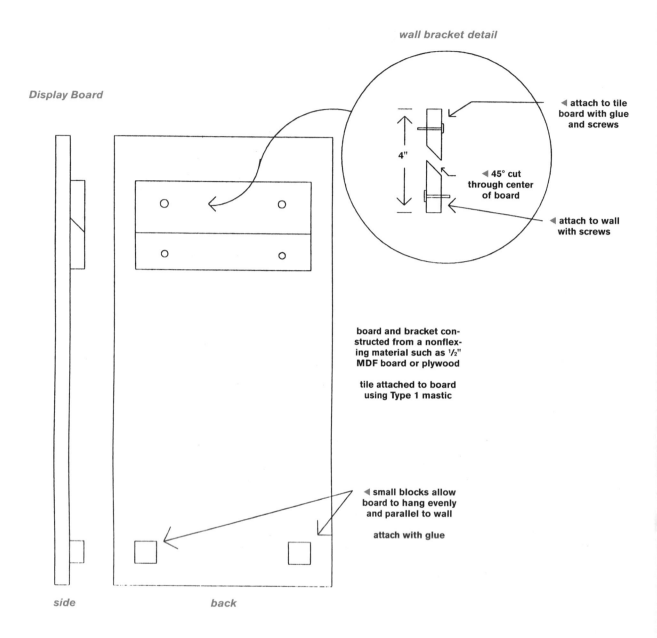

wall bracket detail

Display Board

◀ **attach to tile board with glue and screws**

4"

◀ **45° cut through center of board**

◀ **attach to wall with screws**

board and bracket constructed from a nonflexing material such as ¹/₂" MDF board or plywood

tile attached to board using Type 1 mastic

◀ **small blocks allow board to hang evenly and parallel to wall**

attach with glue

side   *back*

illustration shows an easy way to construct a tile display board. This design can easily be adapted to make the backing for a tile mural.

Your Studio

We all dream of a studio with 10-foot ceilings, walls of windows, and enough room to ballroom dance. The reality of it, though, is that most ceramists try to squeeze their studios in whatever space is available in their already cramped lives. While you can do most tile making in any small corner, there are considerations to keep in mind.

It's important to have at least one window in your work area. Natural light helps you concentrate and is important to your overall mental health. Natural light combined with a good source of electric light helps alleviate shadows and eyestrain. Natural light also helps you see true color. How many times have you selected a color indoors, then viewed it in the sunshine only to discover it looks entirely different?

You also need to consider ventilation. The ideal situation is to have your studio in a separate location away from your living space. Airborne particles of clay and fumes from your kiln become a serious health hazard if they are introduced into your home. If you are using a spare room connected to your home, it's best if the room is on an outside wall with a window or an area where you can vent directly outside. Keep your work area completely closed off from the rest of the house. This includes the clothes you wear while you work. Your clothing will pick up glaze and clay particles, which will drop off as you walk through your home. Always keep a fresh set of clothing available and a separate bag to place your studio clothes in until you are ready to wash them.

Clean greenware and mix glazes outdoors or in a small area separate from your home. Don't use your house vacuum to vacuum your studio. Most vacuums have bags that force air through a filter. Some clay particles are so small they will pass directly through the bag and disperse in the air. Buy vacuum filters rated for small clay particles and look into adapting an old vacuum to accommodate these special filters, then use that vacuum only for your studio. Clean or replace the filter after each use.

Wipe down everything while it is still wet. If you have just finished glazing, wash out the brush while it is still wet. The same goes for every container you mix in. Wipe down the work area after each work session and wash the floor weekly.

Air quality is a big concern for ceramists. Always wear a mask or respirator when dealing with dry compounds. The key to clean lungs is proper equipment and ventilation. Most companies provide a brief description of hazards on the packaging. Contact the manufacturers and compile a folder of all the Material Safety Data Sheets for the supplies you use. This information is important as a reference for proper handling. Keep safety equipment such as a fire extinguisher and first aid kit close at hand.

Never drink or eat in your studio. Clay is very hard on your skin, so take the extra precaution of religiously applying emollients to your hands after washing. Wearing gloves helps, but it's often impractical or unpleasant to wear them for a long period of time.

The key to staying healthy is to realize that although making tile can be fun and exciting, you should always be aware that you are dealing with hazardous materials, and maintaining your health should always be your number one priority. Have your lungs x-rayed on a yearly basis and listen to your body.

Chapter 2

INSPIRATION

Photo by John Carlano.

Melody Ellis, "Hungry Monkey" detail, longhorn red earthenware, cone 05 in an electric kiln.

Where Does Inspiration Come From?

Is your head swimming with ideas one moment and totally blank the next? Could it be possible that your creative spark has fizzled out? Can you force yourself to come up with an idea and be creative? Or does forcing only make things worse? When you do force creativity, you usually find out too late that you wasted time, money, and energy on a project you weren't inspired to do from the very beginning. The key is to get out of the rut and find your inspiration. Where do you go for ideas?

Start by asking yourself what kind of tile you are going to make. Will the tile be decorative or will it be used in a more functional setting? If it's a decorative tile created purely for its artistic

enjoyment, the sky is the limit. Whatever you can conceive, you can create. If the tile is going to be permanently installed in a functional setting, or you are making it for someone else, you should consider a few things before you start the design process. Good sources of inspiration and infor- mation are design and home magazines. They are great visual guides that show what people are putting in their homes.

When creating tile designs, the key is to avoid trends or anything with a heavy theme. Trends come and go, but installed tile will be there for a long time. And remember, if the tile is for you, and you like fuchsia, knock yourself out and make a boatload of fuchsia tile. If the tile is

Common everyday items can be used to inspire entire collections of tile.

for prospective clients, remember that the number one selling tile color in America is white. Yes, white over and over again can be incredibly boring, but if your goal is to market a product, you must consider the consumer. These are things to consider in the future when you start to expand your art to include people other than yourself. For now, you are making tile for the enjoyment of trying something new and creating something with lasting beauty. Not only will you love the final product but you will also enjoy the process of working through what inspires you.

Magazines are useful for a glimpse into home décor as a whole, but they are not the real inspiration you'll be drawing from when you create handmade tile. Once you start designing

handmade tile, you'll see a potential tile in everything from a feather to a fallen leaf. Nature provides us with an endless variety of color, form, and texture. A walk on the beach will provide an abundance of inspiration. The shells, waves, and the movement of the sand will fill your head with ideas. Go out with a paper bag and collect items like leaves, twigs, acorns, pebbles, or shells. Dump your finds on a table and really look at what you've collected. More than likely, you will find inspiration in any one of the objects you've picked up.

Sit outside on a nice day and really look at your surroundings. We move so fast through the day that it appears that everything else is at a standstill. If you take the time to sit still and

Bob Timberlake Collection. Herbs that grow in the summer months inspire "The Summer Collection."

Bob Timberlake Collection. "The Autumn Collection" is based on the most common visual reference of that season – fallen leaves.

Kim Gore, "Grape Vine" tile, 2" x 4".

observe your environment, you will see the abundance of movement, color, and activity that continuously surrounds you. Some of the most beautiful, inspiring actions happen around you every day, but you are moving too fast or are too busy to take notice. A perfect example of applying nature to your everyday life can be found in the work of Bob Timberlake, who has made it his life's work to bring the beauty of nature back into people's lives. His line of tile revolves around the four seasons.

Another great source for ideas can be found in textiles. If you look closely you will notice that the patterns repeat and produce a rhythm. Tile that is installed also has a rhythm running from one tile to another. It is easy to see inspiration in a piece of fabric where there is a bold pattern or color. Color is usually the first thing we notice, followed by pattern, then texture.

When was the last time you were in a city and you looked up? Inspiration abounds on the sides of buildings, especially if the buildings date back 50 years or more. The architectural features that grace older buildings are works of art

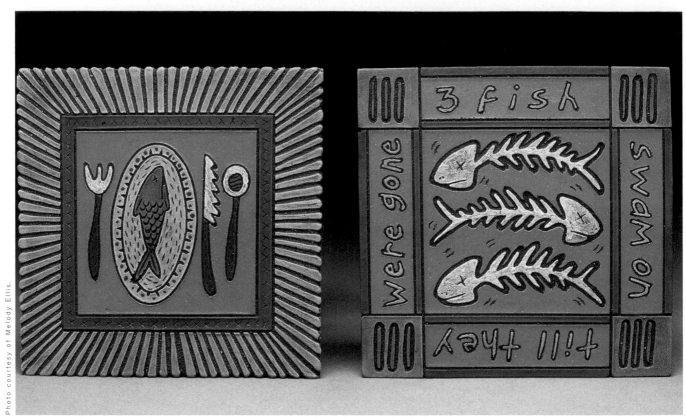

Melody Ellis, "Dinner Tiles," earthenware with underglaze and accented with black grout, cone 05, 5" x 5", 2000.

Yvonne George, kitchen wall installation detail, midrange cone 5 clay with underglaze and sealants.

Susan Werschkul, "Garden Series."

in themselves. For that reason, it is nice to see the efforts being made to preserve their beauty. Next time you're in the city, take a look at the rosettes, friezes, moldings, and bas relief that adorn doorways, lintels, corners, and exterior walls. You can't go wrong with architectural elements – their elegant beauty and style will never go out of fashion.

If you're creating tile for your kitchen, look around your kitchen for inspiration. Open up the refrigerator and take a look at what is in the crisper. You will find apples, lemons, artichokes, herbs, mushrooms, and any variety of beautiful forms. Or look in your china cabinet al the teacups, saucers, silverware, or the simple shapes you find in any vase or bowl. Take a look at the wine bottle and the glass that goes with it, then add a clump of grapes to finish off the series. Nothing is more acceptable or charming than tile with cuisine motifs on a kitchen backsplash.

Remember that although inspiration helps to mold the beginning of an idea, effort will create the finished product.

Chapter 3

Tile Making
TECHNIQUES

Photo courtesy of Bob Jewett, Wilburton Pottery.

Bob Jewett, "Sun Tile," cone 6 stoneware clay with underglaze.

Tile Glossary

As with any vocation, ceramics has a vocabulary. You certainly don't need to memorize the definitions, but I recommend reading through this glossary. It will help you better understand ceramics in general and tile making in particular.

Accent tile. Usually referring to a decorative tile used in conjunction with field tile. Sometimes called a deco.

Bead. A long thin piece of trim usually rounded on top. A bead can be used as a decorative element or to finish an edge.

Bisque. Ware that has been fired once in preparation for glazing.

Brick mortar. Used by brick masons, a coarse thin-set that is well suited for outdoor projects.

Bullnose. A flat tile with one rounded edge, used to finish a row of tile. Also comes as radius bullnose, which has two rounded edges and completes a corner.

Cove base. A flat tile with a curved end used as a transition between the floor and the wall.

Crazing. Spider web cracking that occurs on the glaze surface as a result of tension between the glaze and the clay body.

Cuerda seca. Meaning "dry line," a Spanish method of apply-

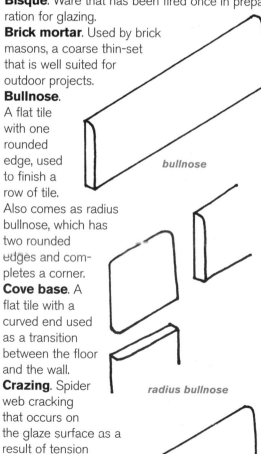

bullnose

radius bullnose

cove base

ing glazes that are separated by a fine line of wax resist. The wax burns off during firing, keeping the glaze separate and the clay exposed.

Delft tile. A well-known traditional white and blue tile originally produced in Holland.

Dot. A dot often refers to a 2" to 3" tile that is placed in a field of larger tiles. The dot is usually in a contrasting color and set between four tiles with clipped corners.

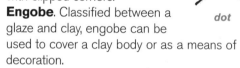

dot

Engobe. Classified between a glaze and clay, engobe can be used to cover a clay body or as a means of decoration.

Epoxy. A thin-set mortar that comes in two to three parts and hardens quickly. It is waterproof and is an ideal adhesive for heavier tile.

Field tile. Flat tile used to cover large areas, usually the background for decorative inserts.

Frit. A frit acts as a flux, which promotes fusion within a glaze.

Greenware. Ware that has not dried sufficiently for firing.

Grog. Refractory material that is ground and added to clay to provide texture, uniform drying, shrinkage, and reduced warping.

Grout. A cement-like product used to fill in the joints between installed tiles. Grout comes in sanded form for wide joints and floor applications, and unsanded for thin joints and wall applications.

Liner. A long rectangular tile.

Listel: A long rectangular tile, sometimes referred to as Listellie, the Italian term.

Majolica. Brightly colored decorated ceramic ware on a white tin glaze field.

Mastic. A ready-mixed organic adhesive that allows tile to be firmly stuck to vertical surfaces without slipping. Mastic does not have the strength or flexibility of mortar but is perfect for applying heavy handmade tile to walls.

Mortar. Also called "thin-set" or "mud," mortar comes in powder form, which is mixed with water or latex additives right before tile application. It is ideal for tiling floors.

Mosaic. Pictures or designs composed of small pieces of just about anything. Traditional mosaics are composed of tile, glass, or pebbles.

Paver. A waterproof unglazed tile made of clay or porcelain. (Some pavers are semivitreous and should be sealed.)

Pug. A charge or lump of clay used for pressing into a mold.

Pug mill. A machine used to mix and compress clay, eliminating the need for wedging.

Saltillo. Mexican red clay tile, usually very soft and not suited for outdoor use. Unglazed saltillo is very porous and needs to be sealed before application.

Sealer. Used to seal porous tile and grout. It is important to use a sealer on unglazed tile or grout that will be subjected to water. Sealing tile allows for easy grout residue cleanup and helps with stain resistance.

Substrate. The underlying structure that tiles are applied over.

Tessarae. Term used to describe the small pieces that make up mosaics.

Undercut. A cut that breaks the vertical line of a design and extends under, creating a ledge.

V cap. Curved tile that wraps around the edge of a counter.

Vitreous. A clay body that has reached maturity by firing up to its highest temperature without deformation.

Wainscoting. The bottom third of a wall, often topped by a chair rail.

Water absorption. The classification of how porous a tile is. Impervious and vitreous tile will absorb little moisture and will handle freezing temperatures. Semivitreous and nonvitreous will absorb moisture and during a freeze the water will expand, cracking the tile.

V cap

Francoise Choveau, "Flora" detail.

Making a Basic Tile

Although the basic process of making handmade tile is similar from artist to artist, the variations on method are a result of the tile artist's experience. Many tile artists find ways to improve on an age-old technique by cutting corners that suit them and their product. The basics become the starting point, while individual techniques are developed over time.

Making sure your clay is the right consistency has a huge impact on the quality of the finished tile. When you open a bag of clay, check how wet it is before you roll the first slab. If you pinch the clay and your finger comes away sticky with clay residue, the clay is too wet and will be hard to handle without disfiguring it when transferring it from one surface to another. Loosely close the bag to allow air circulation, which will evaporate excess water. Remember to check periodically to make sure the clay doesn't get too dry or hard. Pinch the clay between your fingers.

If it feels cool, slightly moist but firm to the touch, it's ready to handle.

Work on a flat level surface with plenty of elbow room and in close proximity to the space where you'll place the completed tile. There is nothing more aggravating than finishing a tile and having to walk across the room to set it down to dry. When your hands are full of wet clay, 20 feet might as well be 20 miles.

Before you begin making your tile, cut two cardboard squares, one $4\frac{5}{8}$" by $4\frac{5}{8}$" and one $2\frac{1}{4}$" by $2\frac{1}{4}$". These are the templates for 4" by 4" tiles and 2" by 2" tiles, factoring in a shrinkage rate of 12%. In woodworking they say, "Measure twice and cut once." This also goes for making handmade tile. What looks like $\frac{1}{8}$" out of square on a wet tile will look like $\frac{1}{4}$" out of square on a finished fired tile. These basic considerations become very important as you move onto more advanced projects. Every tile, whether it is a simple field tile or a blank for a future carved tile, must be square the first time around. So when you measure for the cardboard template, check to make sure all right angles are square.

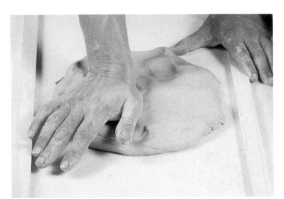

1. Cut a slab from a block of clay, approximately 2" thick. Lay thickness strips on the canvas and place the slab between the strips. Flatten the clay with the heel of your hand.

2. Place a piece of canvas over the slab and roll out the clay, keeping the rolling pin on the thickness strips. Change directions when rolling out the clay. If you always roll in the same direction, the clay particles will lie in one direction, causing your tile to shrink more in one direction than the other and a 4" by 4" tile will be out of square.

3. Remove the canvas and slightly moisten the end of a squeegee, making sure the edge is free of any dried clay or debris. Firmly pull the squeegee over the surface of the clay in one direction to remove the canvas marks.

4. Gently lay the cardboard template on the clay slab. Hold the template firmly against the clay with one hand and use your other hand to hold the pin tool perpendicular to the slab to cut around the template. Pull the excess clay from the tile and run the pin tool around a second time to create a smooth edge. Too-wet clay will pull and distort with the pin tool. If this happens, use firmer clay.

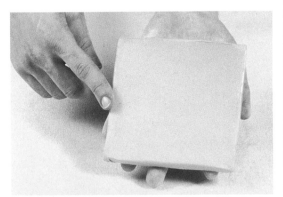

5. Push the tile gently from the side to dislodge it, which will make it easier to lift up without pulling and bending the tile. With a slightly moistened finger, ease the edges to create a more natural corner. Support the tile with your palm and place it aside to dry.

Carved Tiles

Making the basic field tile is an easy first step to making handmade tile. As you move towards decorative tile, you will use this basic field tile as the base of your relief tile. Since your clay body for tile has a lot of grog and sand, you will want to use a smoother clay body if you intend to carve the tile. Remember that a carved tile will be cast, so its firing range or color is not an issue. (You don't want to carve in red clay if you intend to press using white clay. The red clay will stain your tile mold.)

A smooth body stoneware makes a good carving clay. Roll out a slab of clay and let it sit uncovered until the clay is leather-hard (usually about half a day). Keeping it uncovered will get the clay past most of its shrinkage. If you carve on a slab right after rolling it out, it will shrink before you can finish and cast the tile and this shrinkage will affect its final firing size.

After the clay is firm, cut out your tile. This will allow you to work on a surface that has a little resistance. You don't want to move your carving tools over the surface and come away with mush. The leather-hard clay also allows you to mist it during the carving, keeping the surface

Line drawing for tulip design

pliable. Always put the tile in a plastic bag after you are done working on it. Because you have already started drying it out, it will not take long for it to completely dry. Keep the tile covered until you are ready to cast it.

1. Cut two 4½" x 4½" pieces, one ½" thick and one ¼" thick. After rolling the slabs, let them firm up. (This size was determined by the shrinkage rate of the clay.) The finished tiles will measure 4" x 4".

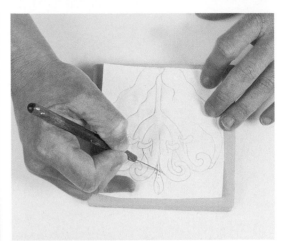

2. Place the line drawing of the tulip on the ¼" thick slab, then trace it with the blunt side of a finger tool.

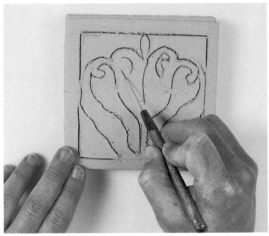

3. Use a potter's needle or finger tool to cut out the design.

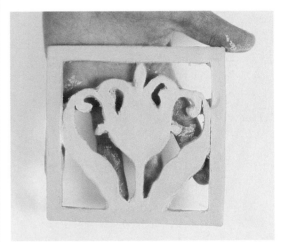

4. Pull away the excess background clay, leaving a clay stencil.

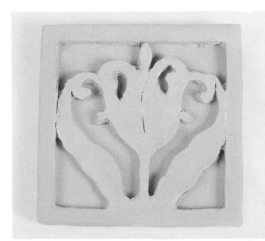

5. Place the stenciled clay on top of the ½" thick slab.

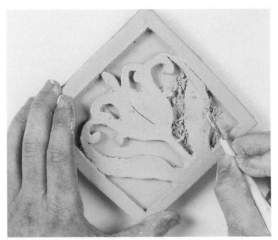

6. By placing the stenciled clay on the slab, you have not only created a smooth background, you have also created the basic relief of your tile. Use a carving tool to carve out the areas of relief. Carve out areas of the leaves to create a rippled edge.

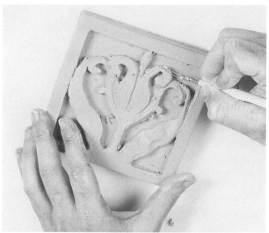

7. Round off the squared edges to create the flower petals.

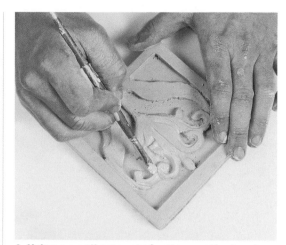

8. Using a small amount of water, run the brush along the seam between the applied design and the tile base.

9. Use a short bristled brush to clean off the tool marks and to smooth out any edges. Brushes make excellent tools when carving tile. I switched back and forth between my tools and the brush, until the tile became smooth, and the detail refined.

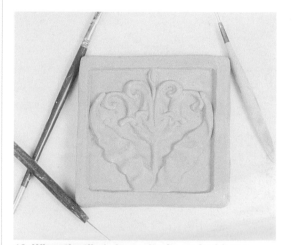

10. When the tile is bone dry, it can be bisque fired. This tile was finished with commercial underglazes.

The tile in the photo was created by first layering a cutout of the basic design, which creates the relief, then carving the detail.

Roll out two separate pieces. Roll the bottom layer, which is the body of the tile, 1/2" thick and the top layer, which will be the relief layer, 1/4" thick. This tile has a 3/8" border around the flower, but you could make the border larger, smaller, or skip it entirely.

Scott Lykens, "Bowling Pins," 6" x 6".

Photo by Scott Lykens, Ohio Style Tile Earthenware.

Drying the Tile

Drying the tile is one of the most important steps in the entire process. If you don't have a good piece of greenware, nothing after this step will improve it. Although there isn't a perfect routine for drying any one tile, there are guidelines that that will make it easier to determine the best drying routine for you.

The first step is to determine your clay body needs. The shrinkage rate of your clay will determine the final size of your tile. To understand how to dry the tile, you will need to understand the drying process.

During the drying process water evaporates from the surface of the tile. When the air holds as much moisture as the clay itself, the drying ceases. That is why air movement, which replaces the saturated air with dry air, is one element in a good drying process. As water migrates through the pores in the clay, the gaps between the clay particles become smaller, which in itself slows down the drying process. A second element is temperature. Even though higher temperature encourages the evaporation of moisture, if the tile is drier than the air, once the heat source is removed, the clay will reabsorb atmosphere moisture until both the clay and atmosphere have equalized. The last (but not least) element in the drying process is the general atmosphere where the tile is drying. Think of the difference of drying tile in a sunny spot on a breezy day verses on a still, humid, overcast day.

I have spoken to several ceramists across

1. When the clay is in its plastic state, the clay particles can move past one another because of the water, which is represented by the small dots in the illustration.

2. Here the clay particles have moved closer together. As they start to touch, the clay becomes leather-hard. There is still sufficient water to allow you to reshape the clay.

3. As the gaps between the clay particles close, it becomes more difficult for the water to migrate to the surface. It is at this point that the drying process starts to slow down.

4. Here the particles have only the smallest amount of water between them. The clay is air-dried.

the country about their drying methods. They've experimented with a variety of techniques with different levels of success. Here in a nutshell is what their experiences and mine have shown.

First, consider the atmosphere where you live. Is your studio located in Virginia, or are you in Nevada? If you live in Virginia, on a sunny summer day the humidity can average 93%. If you live in Nevada, although it is hot, the humidity is in the single digits. This difference becomes important during the first stage of drying. In dry climates, because of the lack of atmospheric humidity, the tile must be covered with plastic the first day to insure that moisture isn't pulled too quickly from the clay, which would cause the edges to prematurely dry and curl. In humid climates, tile can be left uncovered from day one.

Before beginning any part of the tile making process, you must test the clay you are using. This means monitoring test tiles all the way from

5. Here the clay is bone dry, without any water between the particles. This can only be achieved during a water-smoking period. Water smoking, which occurs around 212°F, is when the remainder of the water that was trapped in the clay is driven out by heat.

Helen Weisz, "Dati," 36" x 48".

their moist state through the firing process. Taking the time to test and document your drying results will not only allow you to anticipate your tiles drying time, it will allow you to plan other steps to the process around this downtime. Whatever results you get, if your tile is thicker than the typical ½", you will need to dry it more slowly. The thicker the tile, the more important it becomes to slow the drying process, allowing the moisture to migrate through the large mass of clay. With thicker tiles, it's beneficial and often necessary to cover the clay until it starts to enter its leather-hard state.

There are several options when choosing a drying surface for your tile. You could use anything from open wood racks to expanded metal racks. The cheapest and the easiest drying surface is drywall. No big surprise there – drywall has been used as a surface to dry handmade tile for a long time. You can extend the life of the drywall sheet by taping the edges with a durable tape. Drywall absorbs the moisture from the bottom of the tile while the top air dries. The moisture from top to

bottom doesn't evaporate at the same rate, so if there is a worry about warping, flip the tile after a day or two. Try not to handle your tile too much because every time you touch it you risk breaking it. If your piece is very large and heavy, placing it on a layer of paper instead of directly on the drywall sheet will allow it to shrink and move without pulling or cracking the tile.

Here's a tip for drying your tile more quickly than the three weeks it took me when I first started. Use the clean heat that your kiln gives off to aid drying. Clean heat is the heat generated by the body of the kiln, not the heat inside the kiln being used to fire your tile. *Never use the heat inside your kiln for anything but firing.* The fumes are extremely toxic and should be properly vented to the outside. In commercial tile plants, the heat generated off the kilns is a valuable resource and is utilized to its fullest potential. Place your drying racks in close proximity to your kiln and after a day or two, use fans on a low setting to push the air over your tile. If you do this, you have the three elements to fast dry-

Denni Chiavarini, fireplace detail, geometric and sunburst tile in a 1" x 1" field.

The 4" x 4" field tile on the far left has just been pressed. Notice the difference in the size of the tiles as they go through the stages of production. The wet tile shrinks considerably as it dries. Notice the difference as the tile goes from wet, to bone dry, bisque fired, to glaze fired.

ing – dry atmosphere, heat to encourage evaporation, and moving air to displace the moisture.

Thinner tile will dry more quickly than thick tile but has a greater chance of warping during the drying process. A tile that is too thick could crack if it is dried too fast. Finding that happy balance between the two will take a bit of experimentation. It will not take long to discover what method works, whether it is covering your tile for a day or two, or bringing it closer to a heat source. It will be easier to determine if you make different batches at different times and subject them to a variety of drying routines. Always document your results, taking into consideration any variation from one process to another.

If your tile warps, don't automatically assume that you dried it too quickly or that you used the wrong clay, especially if three out of 10 tiles are warped and the other seven look great. The problem could be how you handled the tile when moving it from one location to another. You will learn that how you handle wet tile affects what the greenware will look like. Clay has what is aptly called "clay memory." When you pick up a tile by the edge and it bends a bit, even though you push it down flat when you place it on the board, two days later the edge you handled may bow up. It reminds me of a dog-eared page in a book. Although the page appears as flat as any other page, once you turn to it you see the crease of the folded corner. One such situation happened to me and I learned a lesson I'll never forget. I was pressing large mural pieces by hand. I cut my blank of clay directly off the pug to be pressed into the mold. Out of 30 tiles, half developed a spiral-shaped crack running through the center. I soon realized that I was taking the cut of clay from the top of the pug, which was the same direction the pug mill had pushed the clay from the barrel.

The spiral ran along where the blades of the pug mill turned. The clay had kept the memory of the pug mill, and where there was stress along the clay particles, it had cracked. The solution was easy enough – I turned the pug on its side and took the cut from the opposite direction. I never experienced this type of crack in my tile again.

When a tile is dry the color will dramatically lighten to an even color from top to bottom. At this stage it becomes greenware.

Greenware might feel dry, but it still retains moisture equal to the moisture in the air. If the tile feels cold to the touch, it probably still has a good bit of moisture in it. It's hard to keep greenware around because it is so delicate. Bisque firing your tile once it is dry will produce ware that is stable enough to easily handle or store. Before bisque firing, the clay should be in its air-dried state, which is the furthest state you can obtain in the open air. Although there is a small amount of water bound within, this is as far as the clay can be dried until it reaches its bone-dry state in the kiln. Bone-dry clay is achieved when your tile is heated to 212°F, the temperature of boiling water. This process is called water smoking. Bone-dry is the state that clay moves into during the early stages of firing. Once it has entered this stage, you should not cool it. If you heat the tile, then take the heat away, the tile will expand as it pulls water from the atmosphere. The stress of expanding will cause cracks and other defects that will show up later.

Keep a piece of dry greenware available and use it as a reference to determine if other pieces are dry. Dry pieces are very brittle and delicate, and need to be handled with care. Should you drop a piece, pick up all the pieces right away. When you step on that little piece it crumbles to dust, which you kick up every time you walk over it.

Chapter 4:

Making a Plaster
MOLD

Kristin Peck, "Medallion," four-piece, stoneware covered in bronze, 6" x 6", Blackwater Tile.

The Original Tile

Making a mold from an original tile is an important step in making reproductions. You can make a mold of just about any tile you produce. If you want to produce multiple 2" field tiles at once, you can make a plaster mold that will yield six or more. It is much easier to press six tiles than it is to measure, cut, and clean six tiles. As long as a tile does not have any undercuts, it can be cast in plaster and then pressed.

Always remember that the subsequent tiles will only be as good as the original. This is the time to check and recheck your tile for imperfections and undercuts. An undercut occurs if the clay is cut under your design, forming a small gap. When you cast your tile, the plaster flows into the gap and forms a ridge that holds the clay in the mold. While further tooling can be done on slight undercuts after the mold is poured, it can be hard to correct large undercuts without distorting the design. As you press your tile you will continuously have trouble with your mold releasing the tile because the clay is caught on the undercut.

To make a mold from an original tile, you will need pottery plaster, a mold-casting frame and clamps, the original tile, a release agent (liquid soap), and a small brush.

It is a good idea to securely cover your tile after it is carved and before it is cast. The longer you leave it exposed to the air the more it will shrink, which will affect its final size. Keep the tile slightly moist in a plastic bag until you are ready to place it in the mold.

Constructing a Mold-Casting Frame

Clamp the mold frame securely together, making a 9" by 9" opening. This is for a 4" by 4" tile. For other tile sizes, having a surround of 2" to 3" is sufficient. Roll some wet clay between your palms to form four small coils to seal the interior of the mold. Lay the coils along the inside seams of the mold frame and with your finger smooth them out to create a seal. The mold holds the shape of the plaster, and the clay coils keep the plaster from leaking out of the frame. Securely clamp the mold frame sides to a smooth surface such as laminate or Plexiglas. Never use a wood surface because the water from the plaster will soak into the wood, causing it to swell.

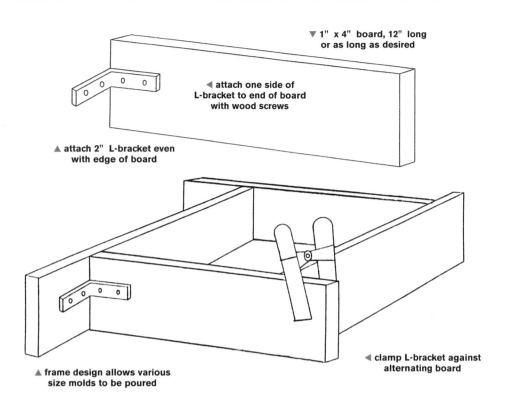

▼ **1" x 4" board, 12" long
or as long as desired**

◄ **attach one side of
L-bracket to end of board
with wood screws**

▲ **attach 2" L-bracket even
with edge of board**

◄ **clamp L-bracket against
alternating board**

▲ **frame design allows various
size molds to be poured**

This diagram shows a simple way to create a mold-casting frame.

Mixing and
Pouring the
Plaster

Brush the interior walls with a light coat of the release agent.

Place the original tile inside the mold frame. If the tile is soft, wet the tile back to create

enough suction to hold it in place. If the tile is leather-hard, lightly scour the back of the tile and wet it. Firmly place the tile in the center of the mold frame and with your palm gently but firmly push down. Give the tile a slight twist to help develop suction between the tile and the table surface. If your tile isn't firmly seated, it will pop up after the plaster is poured. Your tile must stay in place long enough for the plaster to firm up. You are now ready to mix and pour the plaster.

Plaster, which is semi-hydrated calcium sulfate, is an amazing substance that can hold many times its weight in water. Plaster is actually gypsum that has been heated until the water is evaporated. Adding water to powdered plaster will start the crystallization process, and within minutes will cause it to harden. Always use fresh plaster to make molds. Old plaster has had time to absorb moisture from the atmosphere, so it already has a head start on the crystallization process. This means you will have less time to mix and pour.

Important things to consider before you mix plaster are water purity, water temperature, soaking time, and mixing technique. All of these things will have an effect on the pouring time, mold strength, and mold drying time. Water purity

Seneca hand pressed tile.

isn't usually an issue. If you can drink the water, it's clean enough to use in plaster. Substances like organic material or salts affect the efficiency of the mold. Room temperature water works best. If your water comes out of a well, it will probably be much colder than pipes from a city service. Fill a bucket and let it set at room temperature. Cold water will retard the chemical process, while hot water will accelerate it. Always use two buckets when you're doing this, one for mixing the plaster and one that is full of clean water. Use the bucket of clean water to wash your hands after the mold is poured. You will also use this water to dilute the residue plaster in the mixing bucket. This will keep the residual plaster suspended long enough for you to pour it out.

Never pour plaster water down a drain. Although it is wet and doesn't seem like it would cause any difficulty, the plaster will adhere to your pipes and cause major problems. Some companies use 50-gallon drums for wastewater. The plaster particles settle to the bottom and the water evaporates. As they add more and more plaster water, the solids on the bottom accumu-

late and eventually fill the entire container. The container is then disposed of as a solid plaster piece. If you use a plastic container, you could do this with a couple of pourings and then, when it dries, pop it out and dispose of it in a chunk.

When the clean, room-temperature water is ready to be mixed, remember to wear a mask to protect yourself from inhaling plaster dust. I like to wear gloves when I mix plaster because it gives me the chance to find and break any lumps with my hands. You can mix plaster according to a ratio mix specified on the bag or by using the island method. If you are using the island method, you'll have to pay close attention to what is happening on the water's surface. The island method is an easy, no-nonsense method where you add unspecified amounts of plaster to the water. You gradually add plaster to the water, allowing it to absorb, then adding more. Sprinkle a handful of clean fresh plaster over the surface of the water. Immediately after the plaster has settled under the surface, sprinkle another handful of plaster into the water. Continue this until the plaster forms an island that breaks the surface and fails to sink after 10 seconds. At this point, you have added enough plaster. Tap the bucket to force air bubbles to the surface, then stir the mixture. Both the island method and the listed proportion method will give you great results. To save time with future mixings, mark a water line on the mixing bucket. With experience, you will be able to determine the approximate amount of water needed to fill your molds.

What you want out of your mold will determine what your mixture ratio will be. If you want a highly absorbent mold, which will allow your tile to release quicker, you will use more water and less plaster. Your mold will be more absorbent but it will also be much weaker. The higher the plaster ratio, the stronger and less absorbent your mold will be. I recommend starting with the listed proportions and then adjusting the plaster to fit your own individual production.

Water to Plaster Proportions for #1 Pottery Plaster*

Water	Plaster	Total	Cubic Inches
8 oz.	11 oz.	1 lb. 3oz.	20
1 lb.	1 lb. 6 oz.	2 lb. 6 oz.	40
1 lb. 8 oz.	2 lb. 1 oz.	3 lb. 9 oz.	60
2 lb.	2 lb. 12 oz.	4 lb. 12 oz.	80
2 lb. 8 oz.	3 lb. 7 oz.	5 lb. 15 oz.	100
3 lb.	4 lb. 2 oz.	7 lb. 2 oz.	120
3 lb. 8 oz.	4 lb. 13 oz.	8 lb. 5 oz.	140
4 lb.	5 lb. 8 oz.	9 lb. 8 oz.	160
4 lb. 8 oz.	6 lb. 3 oz.	10 lb. 11 oz.	180
5 lb.	6 lb. 14 oz.	11 lb. 14 oz.	200

Water/plaster proportions chart courtesy of the Moravian Pottery and Plaster Works.

* #1 Pottery Plaster is a brand name high quality plaster produced by United States Gypsum Co.

The plaster proportion chart above lists cubic inches. If you are casting a 4" tile, add the measurements of the tile plus 2" all around, giving you an 8" square mold. You then determine how thick you want the mold to be. For this example, let's say the mold is going to be 3" deep. First find the square inches of the mold (8" x 8" = 64 square inches), then multiply 64" by

the required thickness (64" x 3" = 192 cubic inches). Refer to the chart to see that approximately 4 lb. 12 oz. of water and 6 lb. 9 oz. of plaster will give you a total weight of approximately 11 lb. 5 oz.

Sprinkle the plaster over the surface until you notice dry peaks of plaster showing. You will see these dry peaks slowly absorbing water.

After a few moments sprinkle more plaster until the peaks stop absorbing water within a few seconds. This begins the soaking period of the plaster. Not only will soaking remove air from around the plaster particles, it also helps dis-

Lisa Burt, "Majolica Jewels."

perse the plaster. Not soaking the plaster will affect the quality of your mold. Soak the plaster for about a minute and then begin mixing.

For small batches of plaster, hand mixing is ideal. Place your hand in the bucket and fan out your fingers, rotating your wrist back and forth. Try to keep your hand under the surface to avoid trapping air in the plaster. Feel for any lumps and break them up under the surface. You will notice the change in the plaster as its texture changes from a milky consistency to that of heavy cream. When you pull your hand out, the plaster should stick to the hairs on your arm. At this point, you are ready to pour. Lightly tap the bucket on the ground to bring any air bubbles to the surface.

An interesting technique that has produced high quality molds involves a drinking straw.

Mary Collier, "Hand Tile."

Before you start to pour the plaster into the mold, splash a handful of mixed plaster over the tile surface. Use the straw to forcefully blow the bubbles off the tile surface. This thin coating of plaster allows the rest of the plaster to roll over the tile without trapping any air. But be warned, at this point you are working against the clock so if you are going to do this, it has to be done quickly. Keeping the stream of plaster thin while you're pouring will also help break up bubbles.

Pour the plaster in the area between the tile and the mold walls. Pour slowly, allowing the plaster to gently roll over the surface of the tile. A mold that is 2" to 3" thick is ideal. When you are finished filling the mold, pour the bucket of clean standby water into the plaster bucket and set it aside.

Caren A. Goodrich, "Bucking Horse," white clay with commercial glazes, 5¾" x 5¾".

Now is the time to remove air bubbles from the plaster in the mold frame. Bring the bubbles to the surface by *gently* tapping on the work surface. (If you pound on the table too hard, you'll spring a leak.) As the bubbles rise, blow on them to break them up.

Setting and Releasing the Mold

Immediately take care of the excess plaster before it sets up by pouring the excess plaster in a throw-away container to harden so you can dispose of it later. Immediately pour clean water in the plaster bucket to dilute any residue. Pour this also in the waste container and allow the water to evaporate. *Warning:* Avoid contact with your bare skin during the crystallization phase or when the plaster is setting up. During these processes, the plaster will reach a temperature of over 95°F.

You should be able to handle the mold in about an hour. During the recrystallization you will see water accumulating on the surface. Don't remove this water, let it soak back into the mold. It is time to release the mold when the plaster surface no longer has water sitting on top, and the plaster has cooled down. Pull the frame sides away and use a spatula or wire to pass under an edge of the mold to break the suction. Use a blunt object like a wooden sculpting tool

Francoise Choveau, "Elephant and Birds Mosaic," 25" x 19".

to pry a corner of the tile up. You will notice that the tile is softer as a result of soaking up water from the plaster mixture. There is a very good chance that you will not be able to use this tile again, which is all right because the plaster mold gives you the ability to make exact replicas.

The inside edges of the mold will be jagged as a result of plaster seeping between the mold and the tile. Run a flat edge tool or potter's knife along the edge to easily clean it up.

Study the mold before it is dry to see where possible problems might be. You essentially pulled the clay tile out of the mold in almost the same way it would have fallen out on its own. Look for areas where clay may have become stuck or where the original tile might be distorted as a result of pulling against an undercut. Small undercuts are easy to correct while the plaster mold is still soft. Look at the mold from different angles to find undercuts and imperfections.

The bottom of the mold must be flat or it will break during pressing. An unusual but highly effective method of filing the back of the mold is to lay the mold on a flat piece of concrete, flat side down, and firmly grab the edges. Using a push-pull motion, scrape the mold back and forth, wearing it down until it's smooth. This will save you from having to file the back and edges. As you pour more plaster molds, you will learn to easily recognize potential problem areas. File any sharp corners and place the mold on stilts near your kiln or another heat source to accelerate drying. Let it dry completely before using. Using the mold before its time will not only shorten its lifespan, but it will be too wet to release the tile.

There are other mold making materials available on the market, all of which have different properties and different applications. #1 Pottery Plaster is ideal for tile molds because it is highly absorbent and has a compression strength of 2,000 pounds per square inch (psi). Hydro-Stone does not have the absorbency of plaster, but it has a psi of 10,000 pounds, which makes it ideal for using with a manual hand press.

Chapter 5

Using the Plaster Mold to
MAKE TILE

Kim Gore, Medallion Plaque.

Pressing Your Tile

Your mold is done! Now it's time to press the first multiples of your original design. Before you begin, place two ¹/₂" thick pieces of packaging foam on the work surface to cushion the mold. If that's not available, use a few layers of corrugated cardboard. Carefully examine your mold for defects or cracks.

When making clay blanks to produce tile from the plaster mold, the clay consistency is very important. You may have to experiment to find the right consistency. If the clay is too wet it will saturate the plaster and make tile pressing a very slow process. If the clay is too firm it will be difficult to force the clay into the deep detail, which will give you a rather poor copy of your original. You also need to know if the clay

has been de-aired or just mixed. If the clay has not been de-aired, you will need to wedge it, which will take some time. Most clay companies de-air their clay, allowing you to use it directly from the 25 lb. block.

The slab of clay you cut should be ¹/₄" thicker than the deepest part of the mold and fit within the opening of the tile. This extra thickness helps cushion the mold from the force of the mallet when you are pressing the tile. Experience will give you the ability to get the most slabs out of a block of clay. If you plan to do more than one or two copies, take the time to cover your slabs with plastic so they will not dry out before you are ready to press them.

Niki Glen & Helen Helwig, "Harmony, Community, Creativity," glaze and red iron oxide stain, 1998.

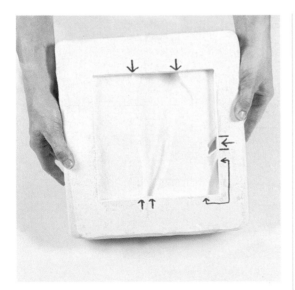

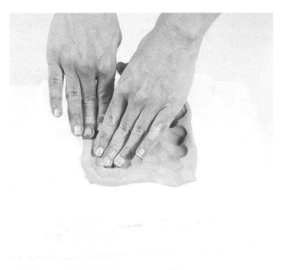

If your mold has any deep recesses, use a pen to mark them on the outside of the mold. Marking the mold will guide you during pressing and releasing the tile. Before touching the inside of the mold, make sure your hands are clean of any creams or oils. Any oil inside the mold will seal the plaster and won't allow the moisture to be drawn out of the clay.

Lay the mold on the padded surface and place the blank of clay directly on top of the opening. Use your fingers to press around the edges, working the clay into the corners. Take notice of the areas you marked as deep relief. In these areas, help the clay into parts of the mold that the mallet will not be able to reach. Press the clay into the corners. This takes a few extra seconds but it insures a nice edge on the tile.

Phyllis Pacin, "Stars and Moons," raku fired tiles, 5" x 4½", 2000.

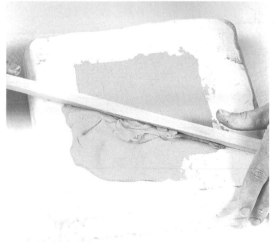

Lay a piece of canvas over the mold. Holding the mallet firmly, start pounding the edges. Hold the mallet at a slight angle when you're pounding the outside edges. This not only helps force the clay into the corners, it also helps avoid chipping the lip of your mold. After the edges are completed, move to the top corner and work your way across and back, covering the entire surface. If your clay is stiff, you will need to use a little more force, especially if the mold detail is deep.

Remove the canvas and use a wire to cut off the excess clay as close to the mold as possible. Starting in the middle of the tile, scrape a lathing strip across the top of the mold, removing the rest of the excess clay.

Photo courtesy of Francoise Choveau.

Francoise Choveau, cement tile, 6" x 6".

Turn the mold around and remove the remaining clay. Always pull from the middle of the tile because pulling from the top will distort the clay in the mold.

If any plaster was scraped off the mold while removing the clay, discard the contaminated clay.

Set the filled mold aside to dry with the clay facing up. It will take between five to 10 minutes to be ready for release. Plaster can hold many times its own weight in water, which is why the clay shrinks in the mold. The water in the clay is being absorbed, shrinking the tile and allowing it to fall out with a little help from you and gravity.

Photo courtesy of Linda Leighton, Higher Fire Clay Studio.

Linda Leighton, stamped image with cobalt oxide and red iron oxide stains and underglazes, cone 6.

As the tile dries, you will see a small crack forming between the edge of the clay and the edge of the mold. When the clay has pulled away from the mold it is time to release it. I don't recommend turning the mold over and letting gravity make it drop out on its own. If the mold is facing up you can keep an eye on it and get the clay out that much quicker when it's ready. Also, if the mold was placed upside down, the thinner area of the tile would release first and the deeper relief could get caught in the mold, causing the tile to tear or warp during the drying process. This is where marking deep recesses on the mold comes in handy. Knowing where relief areas are makes you aware of how you need to handle the tile as it is coming out of the mold.

Photo courtesy of Yvonne George, George Designs.

Yvonne George, "Bluebird," kitchen installation detail.

Hold the mold with both hands with the tile facing down. Gently tap the edge on the padded surface, giving it two firm taps to help dislodge that side of the tile from the mold. Quickly turn to the opposite side and repeat the process. You should see the tile starting to come out on its

own. Tilt the mold down to help ease the clay out. It is always a good idea to let it release slowly, easing it or catching it with your fingertips. The deep areas of the mold might need a little persuasion, which you can do by gently pulling straight down with your fingertips.

Once the clay tile is completely out of the mold, examine both the tile and the mold for any distortions due to undercuts. It is during the first few pressings that a tile mold is refined to produce consistent detailed tile. Should there be any pulled areas on the tile, moisten your fingers and smooth them out. Don't add too much water to the tile because it will remove the fine clay, giving you a groggy surface. If you are careful, you may handle a 4" by 4" or smaller tile immediately after it is pressed, and in doing so clean the bottom edge with your finger. This will eliminate any cleaning you would need to do on the tile after it is dried. Larger tiles must be handled with even more care to avoid warping. A larger tile, or one that is long and thin, should be handled as little as possible after it has been pressed. It can be cleaned after it has firmed up enough to handle,

Photo courtesy of Eric Rattan.

Eric Rattan, "Pine Cone."

within an hour or two, or it can be cleaned after it has completely dried.

Place the pressed tile on a drying surface immediately after it has been pressed. Never walk away from a mold that is waiting to be released. When the tile dries in the mold, it shrinks and cracks the plaster relief.

Should you decide to use the plaster mold to press another tile immediately, it will take a few minutes longer than the first tile did because the plaster loses some of its absorbency with each tile that is pressed. After two or three presses it is a good idea to let the mold dry out a little. As the mold becomes wetter, not only will it take longer to release but it will be weaker as well. Putting the mold on edge in front of a fan or a small blowing heater shortens the waiting time between pressings.

Broken Molds

Eventually you will break a mold. If the mold breaks or cracks during the first casting, you will need to handle it with care so you can put it back together long enough to get at least one pressed tile. Your original tile will have been ruined during the casting so to avoid losing the time it took to create the original, you can attempt to salvage the mold long enough to press one tile and recast it. It will be very hard to put the mold back together if it has broken into more than two pieces, which is why it is so important to press your tile and immediately produce a backup mold in case the original breaks.

Carefully separate the pieces of the broken mold and dry them as you would an unbroken mold. After they are dry, apply common white glue to both sides and strap the sides together. After the glue has dried, carefully scrape the excess away. The mold will be very weak and will only last through one or two pressings, but the goal is to make at least one copy of your tile for recasting. Use a soft brush to gently remove any dust or debris.

Chapter 6

Bisque
FIRING

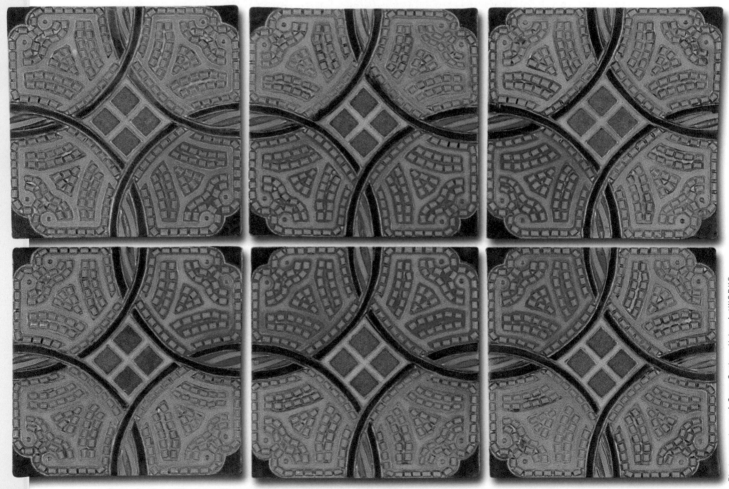

Gary Carlos, "Freeway," earthenware tiles, 11" x 17", 2000.

Bob Jewett, "A Blonde Woman."

The Kiln Log

Taking the time now to start a firing log will save you valuable time later. The example shown is a basic chart that documents information you might want to include in your own log.

Record the date of the firing, which will allow you to determine how many times you have fired in a given period. If you have more than one kiln operating at the same time, assign each kiln a number, then record that number before each firing. Include the cone that you fired the specific load and the amount of time it took for the load to be completed. The comments section is for information that is pertinent to that specific load, whether it is to document

damaged pieces or to comment on an interesting glaze that needs to be duplicated later.

One helpful bit of information that can be gathered from the log is the general condition of your kilns. If you are firing the same cone with the same approximate amount of tile, and you notice that it is taking longer to fire from load to load, your kiln might need a "tune up." A kiln log is also useful in determining the cost involved to fire each load. You'll need to determine the kilowatt usage of the kiln and find out the rate you pay per hour times the hours it took to fire. Keep your kiln log close to the firing area on a clipboard with a pencil attached.

KILN LOG

Date: _____   Kiln: _____   Cone: _____   Time: _____

Comments: _____

_____

_____

_____

Date: _____   Kiln: _____   Cone: _____   Time: _____

Comments: _____

_____

_____

_____

Date: _____   Kiln: _____   Cone: _____   Time: _____

Comments: _____

_____

_____

_____

Date: _____   Kiln: _____   Cone: _____   Time: _____

Comments: _____

_____

_____

_____

Photo courtesy of Caren A. Goodrich.

Caren A. Goodrich, "Grizzly Bear #1," 6" x 6". Modeled in plasteline, then cast in plaster. White clay body with commercial glazes.

Loading the Kiln for Bisque Firing

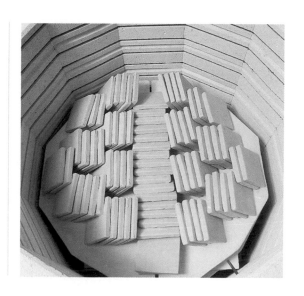

You will be able to fit a lot more tile in the kiln during a bisque firing than during a glaze firing because there's no danger of unglazed tiles fusing together.

There are different ways to load the kiln based on the kiln size, shape, and what you're firing. If you are loading field tiles, you can stack two to three on top of each other at one end of the shelf, almost like a bookend. You then put the rest of the tiles on end, slanting the tiles heavily to one side to allow air to cir-

Linda Leighton, stamped images, cone 6.

culate between them. The rows should be staggered and kiln shelves set wide apart to allow the air and heat to circulate around the tiles. If the tiles are stacked too tightly, the excess density will make it hard for the kiln to reach firing temperature.

If you are loading thick or high relief tiles, make sure they have adequate support along the bottom. Place the first row of tiles on the shelf, then stagger the second row on top. The relief of the bottom tiles will allow for space between the two, enabling heat and air to circulate. If you are firing an exceptionally thick piece, you might want to set it on the shelf without another tile stacked on top. Should the bottom tile explode, more than likely it will ruin the tile that is lying on top of it.

The Firing Routine

The bisque firing is the first firing, which prepares the tile for later glaze application and final firing. Bisque firing creates a porous surface for the glaze to adhere to as well as giving your ware the stability to be handled and set on a shelf for later.

It is very important to make sure your greenware is completely dry before it goes into the kiln. If in doubt, set your kiln on its lowest setting with the lid propped up to allow the last of the moisture to evaporate from the tile. Remember, if you shut the kiln off and don't immediately start the bisque firing, your ware will acclimate and reabsorb atmospheric moisture.

The bisque firing is usually between cone

Sue Werschkul, "Garden Series, Strawberry."

Photo courtesy of Sue Werschkul, Illahe Tileworks.

06 and cone 04. The most crucial stage of bisque firing is the first four hours, where the initial temperature rise must be slow and steady. During the initial stage of firing, the moisture in the clay turns to steam. If the rise in temperature is too fast, the steam cannot escape the ware, which will cause the piece to explode. If your kiln is not vented, the top should be propped open during the first few hours to allow the moisture to escape the kiln.

The type of kiln you have will determine your firing routine. If you have purchased a used kiln and it does not come with detailed instructions, contact the manufacturer for directions for your particular model. Most programmable kilns will already have a pre-programmed bisque firing

ready to go at the touch of a button. Manual kilns should have detailed instructions on the firing schedule for a bisque load.

The routine guidelines for bisque firing dictate a temperature rise of 100°F per hour until 390°F to 400°F has been reached. At this point all the residual water has evaporated and any organic matter has burned off. Ventilation holes can be closed and the temperature rate can be increased to 200°F to 220°F per hour until the cone temperature has been attained.

A bisque load will take between six and nine hours, depending on the density of the ware. With tile, a bisque load is usually very dense so an eight hour bisque fire is not unusual. It could take as long as 13 to 24 hours for a bisque load to completely cool down, again depending on the size of the kiln and the load.

After the firing, you will probably find it difficult to stay away until it is time to open the kiln. Never open your kiln if it is glowing red or orange – this will cause serious damage to the elements and fire brick. The only exception to this rule is during the process used in raku firing. A beginner should never open a glowing kiln unless under the supervision of an expert. If your kiln is a manual, you may open a peephole when the temperature has come down to 752°F. If your kiln is vented, leave it and allow the vent to pull the air through. Once your kiln has reached about 300°F you can open it and take a look at the bisque. The tile will still be too hot to touch even at this temperature. Although the atmospheric temperature in the kiln may say 300°F, the tile is much hotter because it is still releasing the heat that it stored during the firing.

As you unload the kiln, check the tile for defects. If your bisque tile is cracked or bowed, your finished tile will also be cracked or bowed. To avoid the time and money spent working on a bad piece of bisque, cut your losses and throw that piece away or use it as a test tile. If a tile has exploded in the kiln during the firing, thoroughly vacuum the interior, including the elements. Even the smallest shard of bisque can do permanent damage to the elements if it rests there during the next firing.

Chapter 7

Glazes and Surface
TREATMENTS

Kristin Peck, Mermaid, 18" x 18" mural, cone 6, commercial glaze and underglaze.

Linda Warner, "Dragon Tile," underglaze, 6" x 12".

There is a certain freedom when working on a tile. You can paint on it like a canvas or build it up like a sculpture. A tile can be hung on the wall or it can be permanently installed. Depending on what you choose to do with your tiles, the surface will determine their function in your home. The surface treatments are endless and easy to obtain. The following techniques are explained in a simplified manner and should be tried out and explored further. Everything in this chapter can be studied further by reading one or more of the dozens of books that are geared specifically toward ceramic decoration. Glazes or decorative media can be purchased at a ceramic supply house.

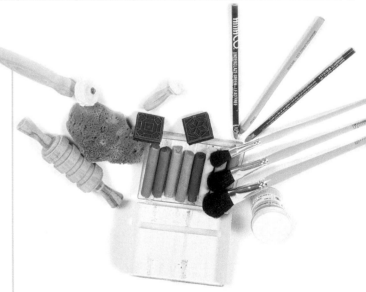

Underglaze

Underglaze is color that is usually applied under the glaze, which makes its use easy to remember. Underglaze colors are made from stains and oxides as well as a small amount of flux. The flux allows the underglaze to bind to the clay body during firing. Underglaze is very versatile and can be applied to either greenware or bisque-fired ware. Applying underglaze to green-

ware tile, then bisque firing, sets the color so you can apply clear glaze without the worry of smearing. If you are applying underglaze to unfired greenware, remember that this is unfired clay and excessive water will muddy the surface. Because the underglaze has not been fired, be careful not to smudge the colors if applying underglaze to bisque ware and then applying a top glaze.

Underglazes come in many forms: chalks, pencils, tubes, pans, and jars. The colors are

Barbara Bloom, "Basket of Spring," white stoneware, underglazes, cone 6.

intense and can be used in concentrated form for detail work or thinned down for a watercolor effect. Because underglazes can be mixed like paint, you can create an unlimited palette. Underglaze pencils have a low flux content that won't fuse to the kiln shelf, so they can be used to mark the backs of tiles. Underglaze pencils also allow you to outline and shade designs as if you were drawing on paper. Most manufacturers rate an underglaze's temperature and any color changes as a result of higher temperatures. Usually unfired colors are close to the final result, which makes using them so enjoyable.

Overglaze

Overglazes, which may be lusters or enamels, are applied over a glazed surface, then fired at low temperatures. They are finely ground pigments that are mixed in an oil-based medium. During the firing, the medium evaporates and the pigment is deposited onto the softened glazed surface.

Overglazes are fired just hot enough to fuse to the existing glaze. When using overglazes on tile, keep in mind that abrasive scrubbing could wear off the overglaze over time.

Overglazes come in bright solid colors, pearls, and metallics. Metallic colors such as gold, silver, platinum, and copper are beautiful but are more expensive. When using a metallic overglaze, don't overlap brushstrokes and don't underfire. If you do either, the metallic will appear dull and lifeless. Always keep in mind that a little overglaze goes a long way and apply it sparingly.

Colored overglazes are mixed with an oil base, which burns off during the firing, depositing the color onto the ware. Metallic overglazes are usually used to rim or highlight particular areas of the design. Lusters, which are also used over glazed surfaces, are iridescent tints of color that are applied over the entire surface with different degrees of translucency.

Glaze

A glaze is simply a layer of glass that is fused to a clay body during firing. It provides a decorative surface and increases the strength of the ware. A glaze allows for a nonporous surface that provides a hygienic covering as well as contributing its beauty by adding color, texture, and shine. Glazes can be sprayed, brushed, or dipped. Once the glaze is applied to the ware and the water evaporated, it actually becomes a layer of powder. During firing the fluxes and stabilizers cause the glaze to turn molten and fuse to the clay body.

Commercially prepared glazes have many advantages, especially for the beginning ceramist. Commercial glazes are prepared under strict conditions and are guaranteed for consistency. There is a huge variety of colors and effects available to the ceramist. Glazes can be purchased in ready-to-use jars or you can purchase glaze in powder form, which has a longer shelf life and takes out the extra water weight, reducing shipping costs. To mix your own glazes from scratch, you would need special equipment and the facility to store the glaze components. If you do want to mix your own glazes, try a simple formula with only a few ingredients to start. (See page 70 for a simple base glaze with added commercial stains to develop a color palette.)

There are more complicated recipes available that yield unique results but require toxic additives. Taking a professional course on handling glaze ingredients will save you time and money in the long run. Please follow the material warnings and handling instructions to the letter and wear protective equipment. Nothing is as important as your health and well being.

gun might have a higher price tag. The glaze, even premixed, should be sieved through an 80-mesh screen. Some premixed glazes are thicker and might need to be thinned down with water. The added water, plus the spraying process, could change the look of the glaze, so test before you spray an important piece.

Gloss glazes come in low-fire and high-fire varieties. Their colors are bright and glossy and they can be sprayed or brushed. The application method does affect the final look of the glaze. Test colors on both a flat surface and a relief surface to decide which technique works best.

There is a noticeable difference in the look of tile glazed with a brush verses one sprayed with a sprayer.

The surface texture on matt glazes ranges from matt to satin. The matt firing range is usually higher than a gloss glaze. A matt glaze can be fired quickly on the way up, but must have a slow cool down to achieve the matt finish. It is hard to achieve a matt finish in a small test kiln because the chamber cools down too quickly and the surface becomes glossy.

Spraying glazes on field tile will give you a smooth and consistent color finish. There are many books on spray booths and spray equipment. Research the equipment and the technique before you invest. A spray gun is relatively inexpensive, but the compressor to use the spray

If you are spraying more than one piece, lay the tile out in rows to form a block. The tiles should be set close together, almost touching. Relief tile should be sprayed from different directions for complete coverage. Positioning the tiles close together stops the spray from reaching the bottom edges, which makes cleaning the bottom of each tile unnecessary.

Check the glaze for its maturing temperature range, which will be listed with the ceramic supply house. Not firing up to the listed cone will give you an underfired surface, resulting in a pitted, gritty, or dull texture.

It's very important that the glaze fit the clay. The glaze and clay must expand and contract within a reasonable range. Should the range of movement be too great between the clay body and glaze, defects in the glazed surface will occur. Basically, if the glaze doesn't fit the body, the two contract at different rates, causing crazing or glaze flaking. Buy a small amount of glaze and test it on the clay for fit before you buy it by the gallons.

Developing Colors

The first step in developing a color palette is to choose a clay body. The color of the clay will have an impact on the final glaze color. Red or brown clay will add warmth to the colors. On these darker clays, yellows and reds will be more intense, while dark blues or purples might become so dark they are indistinguishable. White or buff color clay will allow you to have brighter and clearer colors.

Once you decide on the clay, you will need to develop a test tile. The tile in the illustration is 2" by 3" and approximately ⅜" thick. Incorporate a small relief design to show what the glaze will look like on both a smooth surface and a relief surface. Make a small hole in the top of the piece so it can be hung on the wall. Leave the back unglazed so information related to the firing can be documented. Use an underglaze pencil to record the glaze formula, the cone, and the method of application on the back of the tile.

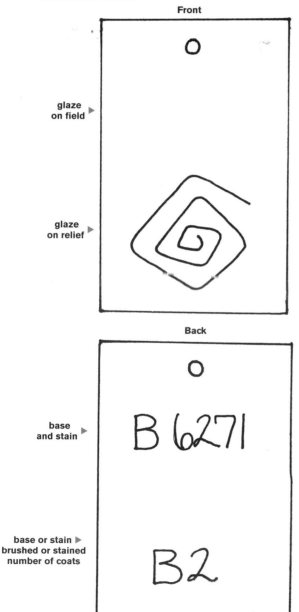

Powdered stains come in a variety of vibrant colors.

To mix base glaze, you will need:
large plastic bag
gram scale
80-mesh sieve
two containers
gloves and mask

One of the easiest ways to develop a glaze is to use a common base glaze and add commercial stains or oxides. The following recipe has a limited number of ingredients, all available at a ceramic supply house. Mix the base in dry form until after adding the colorant, at which point you add water.

The test batch can easily be mixed in 1,000 gram increments, which allows you to mix 10 color batches of 100 grams. Carefully mix each ingredient separately. Place the ingredients together in a large plastic bag. Twist the top securely, leaving air in the bag. Shake or roll to evenly mix the dry ingredients. It is important to get a homogenous mixture.

Cone 6 Clear Glaze Base

30	wollastonite	Used to reduce the shrinkage in clay bodies and glazes during firing
75	frit #3134	A portion of a glaze that has been melted and reground
75	EPK	A type of kaolin, which is a china clay, the purest clay
75	silica	Glassy material that makes up the most important part of a glaze
30	soda feldspar	Used as a flux in glazes
285		

1. Convert the formula to 100 parts by dividing 100 by the total parts (100 ÷ 285 = .351).
2. Multiply each component by the amount from Step #1.

wollastonite	30 x .351 = 10.53
frit #3134	75 x .351 = 26.32
EPK	75 x .351 = 26.32
silica	75 x .351 = 26.32
soda feldspar	30 x .351 = 10.53
	100.02

You now have almost one total part.
3. To make 100 lb., use the numbers from Step #2. To make 10 lb., divide each component by 10 (or move the decimal point left one position). To make a 25 lb. batch, divide each component by 4 (100 ÷ 25 = 4, or for 15 lb. 100 ÷ 15 = 6.667, etc.).
4. To convert a batch to grams, decide how much you want to make and convert the components as follows: (1 lb. = 453.6 grams so to convert from a gram formula, divide each component by 453.6)

10 lb.

wollastonite	1.053 x 453.6 =	477.64 grams
frit #3134	2.632 x 453.6 =	1,193.87 grams
EPK	2.632 x 453.6 =	1,193.87 grams
silica	2.632 x 453.6 =	1,193.87 grams
soda	1.053 x 453.6 =	477.64 grams

I use Mason Stains as the color additive to the base glaze. Mason Stains have been tested for uniformity of color, which is important when trying to achieve consistency. They are readily available through ceramic supply houses across the country and are inexpensive. The stains are listed by number and name, and are mixed directly into the powdered base glaze. Mason also has an extensive color chart and reference guide that is free upon request. This chart lists temperature range, interaction with other compounds, and chemical composition. Other companies also produce stains or pigments. Cerdec, another manufacturer of stains, has a wide range of reds and oranges, which are difficult to achieve. Spectrum also carries a range of stains that work well with base glazes.

Mixing Colors

To mix colors, you will need:
base glaze
gram scale
large plastic bag
spoon
two small buckets
80-mesh sieve
Mason Stain
water
gloves
mask

The basics needed to add color to a base glaze.

In a bowl, measure out 100 grams of the premixed base glaze and place it in a plastic bag.

Measure out five grams of stain color. Start with five grams and adjust according to what you would like your final color to be.

Place the stain in the plastic bag with the dry base glaze and securely close the bag. Roll the bag around to mix the stain and base glaze thoroughly. It is important to completely mix the dry ingredients before adding water.

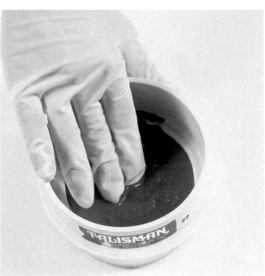

Place the 80-mesh sieve over the other clean container and pour the glaze. Use your fingers to help the glaze through the sieve, removing any lumps and scraping the bottom.

In one of the small containers, measure 115 grams of water. Slowly add the dry mix to the water, saturating the dry particles.

The glaze should be the consistency of heavy cream and can be used to dip, spray, or brush. Always wear a mask and gloves while mixing glaze and remember to record the data. Documentation is the key to developing a consistent and reliable glaze and will allow you to adjust your colors.

Brush or spray the glaze on test tiles. Use different percentages of stain for different levels of color intensity. You can also create your own colors by mixing stains. Document the information on the back of the test tile so you have all the information you need to re-create the color.

Engobes and Stain Washes

Engobes

An engobe is a material that is classified between a glaze and a clay. It has the properties of clay, but is composed of materials found in glaze. Engobes have been a traditional form of decoration for hundreds of years and are still used by potters around the world. They can be used to completely cover a surface or used decoratively as a contrast between the clay body and the engobe itself. An engobe can be used thinned and applied like a glaze, or it can be mixed into a paste and used in building up relief. The characteristics of an engobe fall between a glaze and clay, and engobes are best applied when the ware is leather-hard. Because an engobe is made up of clay, it must shrink at the same rate as the clay body it was applied over.

An engobe can be applied with a spatula and shaped to add texture to the tile or it can be used in sgraffito. For sgraffito, the engobe is applied to the entire surface of a tile, dried to leather-hard, then scratched off with a sharp thin-edged tool.

An engobe is perfect to use in stenciling. You can use leaves, doilies or lace or cut your own stencils. Anything with an open pattern works.

Kristin Peck, "Vineyard," stain wash with top glaze.

Stain Washes

Stains not only work in clay or base glazes, they also work by themselves with a simple medium of water. This is called a *wash*. A stain wash is applied right over the bisque ware and is particularly well suited for a relief tile. Mix the stain with a small amount of water. Always expect to do some testing before you get the results you are looking for. Mix well, because there are heavier particles in some stains that tend to settle to the bottom. Load a mop brush with stain and apply it to the tile. You will notice that the color accumulates in the recessed details of the tile. After the stain has dried, you can either leave it or sponge off the higher points of the tile. This will show the clay body a little more, emphasizing the darker color in the nooks and crannies. You can then spray it with a clear glaze and fire. After a firing, the color will show up darker in the recesses. This technique is sometimes called antiquing.

Surface Decoration

Sprigging

Sprigging is adding low relief decorative objects to an already existing clay form. Wedgwood, with its trademark blue and white decoration, is a good example of sprigging. You can hand form or press mold a decorative feature and join the two pieces with slurry or slip. This technique can be used with different color clays or different clays altogether. If using different clays, make sure the two have the same shrinkage rate.

The tiles on page 75 were made from a seashell that was molded and cast. The shell was pressed into a piece of clay, bisqued, then used as a mold to make exact replicas. Or you can cut a thin slab with a cookie cutter or template and, with a little modeling, make a sprigging decoration. Cookie cutters work well and can be found in anyone's kitchen drawers, bakery shops, garage sales, or discount stores.

These 2" x 2" tiles are sprigged with seashells pressed from a bisque mold. The mold was created from real shells pressed into clay and then bisqued.

Wax Resist

Wax resist, available at ceramic stores, can be applied to tile to prevent colors from mixing together. Applying it to your tile will prevent glaze or slip from adhering to selected areas. Whatever is under the wax will show up after the firing. The wax burns off and doesn't leave a residue, and works great as a stenciling technique. Wax resist can be applied with a brush, which can cover large areas, or it can be purchased in a pen form for fine detail lines. A more economical method for achieving fine detail would be to purchase a refillable bottle with a fine tip.

Stamps

Clay that is slightly firm is ideal for stamping. Don't stamp clay that is too wet, or the stamp will leave a muddy impression. Stamping on tile is a relatively simple procedure because the tile is already laying flat. The key to stamping is keeping the stamp level and the pressure even. Once you have pressed the stamp down, raise it straight up to avoid smearing the design.

A stamp can be made from just about anything. It can be wood, plastic, rubber, ceramic,

organic, or anything that leaves an impression. Objects that you have around your home make great stamps – children's alphabet blocks, washers, bolts, forks, buttons, bottle caps, paper clips, wrinkled plastic wrap, or even just your thumb.

Wood stamps can be bought or easily made by cutting a simple design in the end grain of a dowel rod. You might even paint the end with underglaze or engobe and press in the design and color at the same time. Wood or plaster blocks can also be carved for larger, more intricate designs. Dense foam can be carved, glued on a wood platform, and used to impress a design.

Ceramic bisque stamps are easily made and can be used over and over again. Make a thick cylinder from a piece of clay. Press one side of the cylinder down to flatten it. Then carve the design or press a small object into the flattened end. Put the piece aside until it is completely dry, then bisque fire. You now have a stamp that won't stick to your clay and will last forever. Some ceramic artists have a library of hundreds of stamps they have made.

Organic materials like leaves or flowers can be rolled onto your clay slab to create an impression. To make a clear impression with leaves,

These 2" x 2" tiles are pressed with small stamps made of bisqued clay.

they should have heavy veining, which should be placed face down on clay. For variety, roll out a solid piece of clay with a continuous design on it. Fish netting, burlap, or a wrinkled paper bag make interesting impressions. After the design has been pressed, cut out the tile. Lace or doilies can be rolled onto clay with wonderful results, especially if the design is later emphasized by adding a stain wash.

Artists who want to use ready-made stamps can purchase commercial stamps at craft stores. They come in a variety of forms, from rubber to hard plastic, roll-on or press. They offer variation and instant gratification at a reasonable price. Craft stores also sell ink stamps in any shape imaginable. Just make sure the design is deep enough to make a good imprint on the clay.

Inlay

A tile can be inlaid with either clay or glass. Each requires completely different techniques and materials.

Inlay using multicolored clays is easy and

very effective. While the tile is leather-hard, lightly trace a design on the surface. With a sharp modeling tool, cut deep grooves around the design. Use different colored clay pieces to form a small coil. Lay the coil in the cut grooves. Firmly press the coil into the recessed areas, completely filling them. Scrape away the excess with a metal scraper by dragging it across the surface until the inlay design is crisp and the colored clay is cleaned off of the surrounding surface.

Inlay or fusing with glass is a bit more complicated. It is important to research the technique before you attempt it. In fusing, crushed glass is placed into the recessed areas of the tile, so designing a tile with recessed areas that have straight walls and consistent recessed depth is important. The walls keep the glass from flowing out onto the tile or into each other. The crushed or powdered glass is called frit, and it is available in most ceramic catalogs. Remember that the firing schedule for glass is completely different than for ceramics and is very important in the glass fusing process.

Chapter 8

Glaze Firing the
TILE

*Eric N. Rattan,
"Autumn Color III,"
1,000 piece handmade
floor tile faux carpet
mosaic, 2001-2002.
Heritage Foundation
Award.*

Photo by Skot Weidemann.

Kim Gore, "Grape Vine Wine Table."

Firing Methods

For the purposes of this book, the use of an electric kiln is assumed. Even though electric kilns are the most readily available to the general public, there are other methods of firing that should be discussed. Knowing your options will allow you to push your interest farther. Although practice makes perfect, it is experimentation that opens the door to new and exciting results.

Raku is a low-fire technique where the piece is taken out of a red-hot kiln and placed in a chamber filled with combustible material. The results are striking in color and pattern movement. Raku is a Japanese word loosely translated to "enjoyment," which aptly describes the results. Raku firing requires special clay, one that can withstand the shock of radical temperature changes. To get the range of color during a raku firing, glazes must be specially formulated to achieve the range of intensity and metallic hue. Although raku tiles are beautiful, something must be said about their durability. The finished pieces will be porous and the surface difficult to clean. The glaze may contain toxic ingredients, so the tile's function

must be considered before it is installed. Even properly sealed, raku tiles should not have any contact with food. Raku tile would be perfect in a fireplace surround or in any decorative setting. Because it is a low-fire tile, it will also be a bit weaker than a higher fired tile. Apply a sealer to the tile and it will not only stop any harmful residue from leaching out, it will help maintain the colors. Raku has been known to change color over time because the metallic finish oxidizes when exposed to air.

Sagger and **salt firing** are two other firing techniques that are used by tile makers to produce beautiful results. Sagger is actually the name for the box that is put inside the kiln to separate the ware from the heat source. Saggers are made of refractory material, the same stuff your kiln shelves are made of. Saggers are stacked on top of each other in the kiln and the tile is placed inside, arranged tightly with a packing of sawdust. This technique is used at the Moravian Tile Works, giving a smoky finish that greatly enhances the pieces. Salt firing originated in Rhineland and was achieved by using common salt during the

Phyllis Gillispie, "Finial," ceramic with copper metal and patina finish.

firing. A salt glazing kiln must be very well vented and once used for this technique cannot be used for any other kind of firing.

Using an electric kiln will give you the most consistent colors and results. The atmosphere in an electric kiln is called oxidation – when air has access to your firing chamber during the entire firing process. With an electric kiln, glazes are usually smooth and color consistent.

Commercial glazes are available that have been carefully developed to mimic reduction glazes, the glazes that are used in gas-fired kilns to create heavy texture and color pattern. Commercial oxidation glazes are designed to look like a reduction firing, encouraging the same texture and color intensity you would get from a gas kiln. If there aren't any reduction colors available that fit your needs, you can encourage texture by layering different glazes on top of one another. Remember that when you manipulate any technique, you encourage individual character.

Equivalent Temperatures (F)
For Orton Pyrometric Cones

Cone	Self Supporting Cones						Large Cones				Small
	Regular			Iron Free			Regular		Iron Free		Regular
	Heating Rate F/hour (last 180F of firing)										
	27	108	270	27	108	270	108	270	108	270	540
022		1087	1094				N/A	N/A			1166
021		1112	1143				N/A	N/A			1189
020		1159	1180				N/A	N/A			1231
019	1213	1252	1283				1249	1279			1333
018	1267	1319	1353				1314	1350			1386
017	1301	1360	1405				1357	1402			1443
016	1368	1422	1465				1416	1461			1517
015	1382	1456	1504				1450	1501			1549
014	1395	1485	1540				1485	1537			1598
013	1485	1539	1582				1539	1578			1616
012	1549	1582	1620				1576	1616			1652
011	1575	1607	1641				1603	1638			1679
010	1636	1657	1679	1600	1627	1639	1648	1675	1623	1636	1686
09	1665	1688	1706	1650	1686	1702	1683	1702	1683	1699	1751
08	1692	1728	1753	1695	1735	1755	1728	1749	1733	1751	1801
07	1764	1789	1809	1747	1780	1800	1783	1805	1778	1796	1846
06	1798	1828	1855	1776	1816	1828	1823	1852	1816	1825	1873
05½	1839	1859	1877	1814	1854	1870	1854	1873	1852	1868	1909
05	1870	1888	1911	1855	1899	1915	1886	1915	1890	1911	1944
04	1915	1945	1971	1909	1942	1956	1940	1958	1940	1953	2008
03	1960	1987	2019	1951	1990	1999	1987	2014	1989	1996	2068
02	1972	2016	2052	1983	2021	2039	2014	2048	2016	2035	2098
01	1999	2046	2080	2014	2053	2073	2043	2079	2052	2070	2152
1	2028	2079	2109	2046	2082	2098	2077	2109	2079	2095	2163
2	2034	2088	2127				2088	2124			2174
3	2039	2106	2138	2066	2109	2124	2106	2134	2104	2120	2185
4	2086	2124	2161				2120	2158			2208
5	2118	2167	2205				2163	2201			2230
5½	2133	2197	2237				2194	2233			N/A
6	2165	2232	2269				2228	2266			2291
7	2194	2262	2295				2259	2291			2307
8	2212	2280	2320				2277	2316			2372
9	2235	2300	2336				2295	2332			2403
10	2284	2345	2381				2340	2377			2426
11	2322	2361	2399				2359	2394			2437
12	2345	2383	2419				2379	2415			2471
13	2389	2428	2458				2410*	2455*			N/A
14	2464	2489	2523				2530*	2491*			N/A

These tables provide a guide for the selection of cones. The actual bending temperature depends on firing conditions. Once the appropriate cones are selected, excellent, reproducible results can be expected. Temperatures shown are for specific mounted height above base.

Chart courtesy of Orton.

What Is a Cone?

A cone is a tapered three-sided pyramid designed to indicate the temperature within a kiln. Cones are designed to soften and bend at various temperatures. The word cone is used to designate the temperature a kiln is being fired to. For example, firing to cone 6 means you are firing to 2232°F.

Cones come in two different sizes. The senior, or self-supporting, cones are used in monitor-ing the firing. They are placed in front of the peepholes so they are visible from the outside. They are either self-supporting and stand on their own or they fit in a specially designed holder.

The smaller cones, called junior cones, are used in conjunction with a kiln sitter. Your kiln should have a kiln sitter and a limit timer. A junior cone is placed between the three bars on the kiln sitter and bends when the desired tempera-

Equivalent Temperatures (C)
For Orton Pyrometric Cones

Cone	Self Supporting Cones						Large Cones				Small
	Regular			Iron Free			Regular		Iron Free		Regular
	Heating Rate C/hour (last 100C of firing)										
	15	60	150	15	60	150	60	150	60	150	300
022		586	590				N/A	N/A			630
021		600	617				N/A	N/A			643
020		626	638				N/A	N/A			666
019	656	678	695				676	693			723
018	686	715	734				712	732			752
017	705	738	763				736	761			784
016	742	772	796				769	794			825
015	750	791	818				788	816			843
014	757	807	838				807	836			870
013	807	837	861				837	859			880
012	843	861	882				858	880			900
011	857	875	894				873	892			915
010	891	903	915	871	886	893	898	913	884	891	919
09	907	920	930	899	919	928	917	928	917	926	955
08	922	942	956	924	946	957	942	954	945	955	983
07	962	976	987	953	971	982	973	985	970	980	1008
06	981	998	1013	969	991	998	995	1011	991	996	1023
05½	1004	1015	1025	990	1012	1021	1012	1023	1011	1020	1043
05	1021	1031	1044	1013	1037	1046	1030	1046	1032	1044	1062
04	1046	1063	1077	1043	1061	1069	1060	1070	1060	1067	1098
03	1071	1086	1104	1066	1088	1093	1086	1101	1087	1091	1131
02	1078	1102	1122	1084	1105	1115	1101	1120	1102	1113	1148
01	1093	1119	1138	1101	1123	1134	1117	1137	1122	1132	1178
1	1109	1137	1154	1119	1139	1148	1136	1154	1137	1146	1184
2	1112	1142	1164				1142	1162			1190
3	1115	1152	1170	1130	1154	1162	1152	1168	1151	1160	1196
4	1141	1162	1183				1160	1181			1209
5	1159	1186	1207				1184	1205			1221
5½	1167	1203	1225				1201	1223			N/A
6	1185	1222	1243				1220	1241			1255
7	1201	1239	1257				1237	1255			1264
8	1211	1249	1271				1247	1269			1300
9	1224	1260	1280				1257	1278			1317
10	1251	1285	1305				1282	1303			1330
11	1272	1294	1315				1293	1312			1336
12	1285	1306	1326				1304	1324			1355
13	1310	1331	1348				1321*	1346*			N/A
14	1351	1365	1384				1388*	1366*			N/A

For Self Supporting -1fl; for Large - 2"; for Small - ¹⁵/₁₆". For Large Cones mounted at 1³/₄" height, use Self Supporting temperatures.

* These Self Supporting Cones and Large Cones have different compositions which result in different temperature equivalents.

ture is reached; it then shuts off your kiln. The limit timer is your backup safety and is set a short time past how long you expect the firing to be. It will terminate the firing if the cone does not bend or the sitter malfunctions.

If you are questioning the accuracy of your kiln, using cones to monitor the temperature is your best solution. Use a cone representing the desired temperature, one cone number higher, and one cone number lower. Place them on the top shelf, middle shelf, and bottom shelf. The kiln should be loaded with the same amount of density as a typical firing. After the firing is complete, you will be able to visually determine if the firing temperature was even from top to bottom.

The senior cone sits in a clay cone sitter, while the junior cone will be placed in the kiln's cone sitter.

If you're lucky enough to have an automatic kiln, you will have a small instruction manual to read, a few buttons to push, and you're ready to fire. If your kiln is manual, you will have to pay more attention to the time period between increasing the temperature and venting. Either way, you should always know the basics regarding what's going on in your kiln during the firing.

Loading the Kiln

Unlike bisque firing, during a glaze firing your tile cannot be stacked. If you were laying tile flat on kiln shelves, it would seem a good idea to utilize the space by placing the shelves close together. In reality, you will not be able to get them too close because of the excessive density. Too much in the kiln does not allow the kiln to reach its higher temperatures and will add significant wear and tear on your elements. After a firing or two, you will be able to determine how many shelves you can fit in the kiln with all of the tile reaching maturity.

A common problem with kilns is a cold spot near the bottom of the kiln. The exception is if your kiln has elements in the bottom. If you don't have the extra elements in the bottom of your kiln, it can be as much as 25°F cooler, which translates into a half a cone or more. You can work around this problem by elevating the bottom shelf 3" to 4" off the kiln floor. Remember, the closer the shelves are, the longer the firing will be. Keeping them evenly spaced allows heat and air to circulate, which prevents overworking the kiln.

Most ceramists, including tile makers, use kiln shelves. There are other alternatives, but they require an investment, and it's always wise to try every alternative before you invest. If you are using kiln shelves, make sure the shelf is rated for the temperature you intend to fire to. I was using a top quality, heavy-duty kiln shelf until I read an article in an industrial ceramic magazine about the California power crunch. Industrial ceramic companies were crying over energy and production costs. When the experts came in, one of their suggestions was to replace their heavy-duty kiln furniture with cheaper, lighter shelves. Because of the lack of density, the kiln had less to heat and used less power. I replaced my shelves with lighter, less expensive shelves and took an eight and one-half hour firing down to seven hours. You are not only firing the tile, you are firing the shelves. There is a risk in going with cheaper shelves, so understand them before you switch. The lighter shelves cannot support excessive weight, and they are a bit more brittle. Your tile may not be too heavy, but pots or sculpture could be. After firing make sure there aren't any hairline cracks running through the shelves. Thinner shelves tend to bow, which you can compensate for by flipping them over and using the other side.

Flipping shelves brings up another issue – kiln washing. Should you kiln wash? If you kiln wash and flip your shelf, you will definitely find chips of white flake on the tile after it is fired. However, there are situations where it is necessary to kiln wash your shelves. If you are using a community kiln, you should kiln wash. You might be fanatic about a clean tile bottom, but don't expect everyone else to be. If you are glazing pots or any vertical surface along with your tile, then kiln wash. Gravity and the flow of glaze have been known to puddle on the base of a pot now and then. If you are dipping tile completely into the glaze, then kiln wash the shelves. It is impossible to get all the beads of glaze off every tile.

If you are spraying or brushing and the kiln is only used by you, then don't bother with the kiln wash. Out of the hundreds of thousands of tiles I have glazed, I have never had to pry a tile off a shelf, but I did have to throw a bunch away because the surface was contaminated with kiln wash. After a time the wash gets brittle and pops off. If you lay a tile on the shelf and push it across the surface, you can see the wash flake off and pop onto a tile 4" or 5" away. The only time I have discovered glaze on a shelf was when I let someone else use my kiln. Like I said, no one will be as careful as you are.

The way you load your kiln with tile is a matter of trial and error. Here is a suggestion, but try it before you commit. Because gloss glazes tend to fuse faster and harder together than matt glazes, this technique is best suited for tiles glazed with a matt glaze. Since the key is to fit as many tiles on the shelf as possible, experiment with this idea. If you are using clay with a high shrinkage rate, place two glazed tiles on the shelf so they are touching. If this doesn't work, the worst that will happen is that you will have sacrificed two tiles, so make sure they are scrap or test pieces. Fire the tiles and see if they become fused together or if they fire without any problems and there is a slight gap between them. This goes against all glaze-loading principles but it does work in some cases. Although the tiles are touching before the firing, during the firing and before the glaze starts to melt, the tile shrinks, creating enough space between the two so they do not become fused. This will not only allow you to squeeze an extra tile or two on the shelf, it will cut out the tedium of checking to make sure the tiles aren't touching each other. Remember, test this method before you sacrifice any good tiles. Every method has many variables, and it's up to you to test with your specific conditions to find out what works for you.

What Goes on During Firing?

After a time you will be able to visually determine what is going on in your kiln. The color in the kiln gives you an idea of what the interior temperature is. At the beginning of the firing, the kiln interior takes on a dark red glow. At this point, the kiln temperature is around 1000°F to 1100°F. As the temperature increases, the color changes from orange to yellow to bright white. At the bright white stage, the kiln temperature is around 2300°F or hotter. Never look directly into the kiln, especially when the brightness intensifies. Always wear protective eyewear or you will damage your eyes.

Yellow Heat

Porcelain
Stoneware
High-fire Glaze

Orange Heat

Bisque
Low-fire Glaze

Red Heat

China
Lusters
Gold
Glass

Vitrification starts
and continues

1000

Fusion starts

700

Ceramic change
and decomposition

Drying

120

CONE

10
9
8
7
6
5
4
3
2
1
01
02
03
04
05
06
016
017
018
019
020
021
022

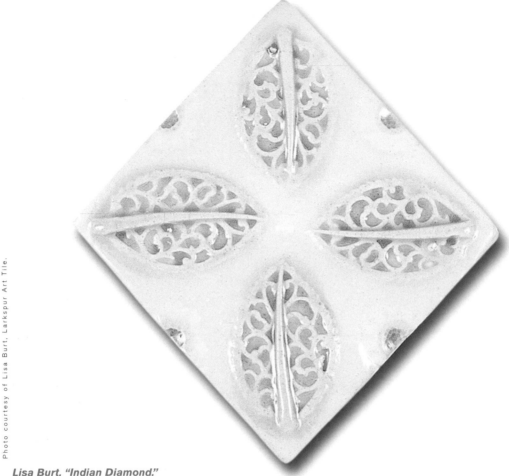

Photo courtesy of Lisa Burt, Larkspur Art Tile.

Lisa Burt, "Indian Diamond."

The chart shows the rise in temperature in correlation with the change in color. The chart also illustrates the corresponding cone number relative to color, and the changes and functions that occur during that temperature range.

For the best results during glaze firing, make sure the glaze works with the clay. If you are using cone 5 glazes, use cone 5 clay. The compatibility of the two will prevent a lot of problems that aren't noticeable until after the glaze firing.

Every kiln is different, based on the variables of your firing, including the age of the kiln, the density of the load, how high you are bringing the temperature, and the effect you want to achieve. Read the kiln manual before you fire or, if you are using a community kiln, ask what their firing profile is. There are many books dedicated to the use and theory of electric kilns and they are definitely worth a look.

While the bisque firing needed a slow increase in temperature to eliminate moisture and organic matter, the glaze firing can ramp quickly. But opposite of the quick cool down in a bisque firing, a glaze cool down must be much slower. In some glazes, the characteristics of the glaze develop during the cool down period. While the rate of temperature climbs faster during a glaze firing, be aware that the hotter the kiln gets, the slower that rate of climb will be. If your kiln has a motorized vent, all the peepholes and the kiln lid will be closed throughout the entire firing. If your kiln is manual, you will have to prop the lid or keep a peephole open. Also, your kiln must be in a room that is adequately vented and away from anything that needs clean air to breathe. The fumes given off during a glaze firing are very toxic.

The hardest thing about using a kiln is waiting until it is cool enough to open. Opening your kiln prematurely may crack the tile and more than likely craze the glaze surface. Wait until your kiln is 130°F or less, then open the kiln and take out the tile. The tile and kiln shelves will still be hotter than the atmosphere, so wear gloves.

In most cases the glaze firing is the second and final firing, but if you apply overglaze, you will need to do a third firing.

Chapter 9

Home Décor with
TILE

Gary Carlos, "Youth Voices" detail.

When you design tile, the easiest way to approach it is to look at each piece as a component of a larger piece. If you are creating a series, all the pieces should work with each other or at least carry a common theme. For example, if you wanted to design a series around the seasons, you could choose motifs from the different times of the year such as tulips, daffodils, or birds for spring and leaves, gourds, and wheat for autumn, etc. Along with your design you could also use colors that correspond with the season – yellow, pink, and green for spring; red, orange, and gold for fall. When choosing a theme or design, keep in mind the permanence of a tile installation and how it will affect the rest of the room.

Barbara Bloom, "Rainbow Road," white stoneware, cone 6, underglazes.

Photo courtesy of Barbara Bloom.

Tile Installations

You have two alternatives when doing a tile installation. You can either make the decorative tile and surround it with store bought tile, or you can tackle the entire job and make it completely out of handmade tile. If you are going to make only the decorative tile, you will need to make tile the same size as the commercial tile. Sizes vary, but a 4" commercial tile is usually 4¼". There will also be a difference in thickness because commercial tiles are produced mechanically and are very thin, while handmade tiles are thicker out of production necessity. It looks nice to have the handmade tiles protrude from a field of commercial tiles, but you must remember to glaze the edges of the handmade tiles so bare clay is not exposed after they are mounted. Using commercial tiles to surround your handmade tiles is an inexpensive way to get a designer look without putting the effort into making the total square footage.

Below is an approximation of how many tiles you will need to cover one square foot.

Most listels or tiles that are used as borders and trim are measured in linear feet. If you have a 2" by 6" tile and need to border a 10 foot kitchen, you would need at least 20 pieces plus a few extra for breakage or any other mishap that might occur.

Although it sounds like a good idea to complete the entire job with handmade tile, study the numbers before you tackle the job. If you have a backsplash that is 2 feet by 10 feet, you have 20 square feet to cover. Twenty square feet of 4" by 4" field tile, with nine tiles per square foot, will equal 180 4" by 4" tiles, with at least 10% added for waste. Finish making the new tile before you take the old stuff down or put any area in your house out of commission. It could take a while to complete a large job if you don't have much time or kiln space.

Size of tile	Needed to cover one square foot
4" x 4"	9
2" x 2"	36
6" x 6"	4
8" x 8"	2¼
2" x 6"	12

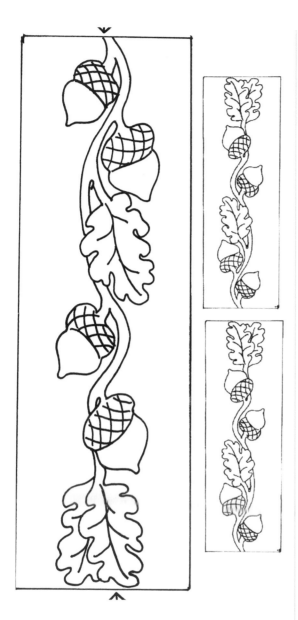

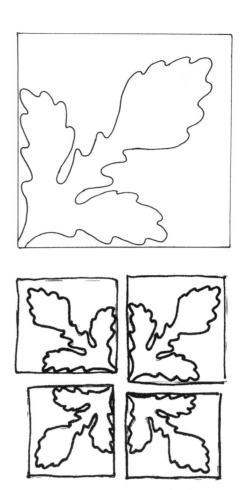

The two illustrations above show how easy it is to use a simple 4" by 4" design to create a large 8" by 8" tile mural.

When you are designing tile, remember that you will lose tiny details. Also consider where you intend to use the tile. If you design tile with high relief, you will not be able to use it on the floor. Since you will be making multiple tiles from a tile mold, use your first few pieces as test pieces to try out different glaze colors. Never fall in love with a piece until it is out of the kiln. If you have a tile job that calls for 25 pieces, make 30 just in case. There are a number of things that can go wrong and having those extra pieces will save you time and money.

If you are doing a large job, mix the amount of glaze you will need for the entire job. Mixing a small amount in one sitting, then later mixing more could cause a problem with color matching. The slightest variation from one lot of tile to the other will result in a variation. If consistency of color or detail is important, you should complete the tile as a batch.

In these illustrations, you can see how the listel was designed to flow from one edge to the other. An easy way to do this is to place a repeating connection between the tiles. This way, no matter how the design ends, the tiles will match up. You can also make a 2" by 2" connector tile using a simple element, in this case an acorn, and produce a tile that plays off the larger design.

Expanding a design is easy if you remember to keep it symmetrical and avoid making it obvious what is the top and what is the bottom. The 2" by 2" acorn can be installed on the square (straight up and down), or it can be turned at an angle and used in a diamond pattern.

Motifs

It is amazing how you can utilize simple forms to create outstanding tile. One motif that is a favorite of tile designers is the acanthus leaf. It can be seen throughout history as a favorite subject for three-dimensional decoration. It seems that every period in history featured a favorite version of this leaf. Today's designers have toned down the swirls and intricacies of the acanthus leaf and adopted the attitude that simple is better.

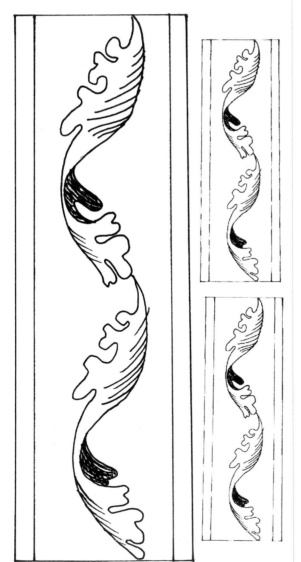

The listel tile shows a simplified version of an acanthus leaf. You can see how the leaves flow from one tile to another without seeming to break rhythm. The second illustration gives you an idea of what these tiles would look like set side by side.

The pattern on page 89 would yield a 6" by 6" tile, accounting for 12% shrinkage. It is a medieval design that can be used on its own or incorporated into a four-piece medallion.

This grape cluster pattern on page 90 with a twist will also yield a 6" by 6" tile. Notice the vine design that runs along the top of the tile. This element can be used to link two or more of the same tiles together, creating a continuous row of cascading grape clusters suspended from a grape vine.

Installing Tile

The information that follows briefly describes materials and tools that are used during tile installation. There are many books and videos available on tile installation that should be considered before you start installing your tile, especially if you have never done it before. Follow the guidelines laid out by Tile Council of America (see page 86) for basic installation procedures. Remember that if you are installing tile in certain areas, it might render that area out of commission until the job is complete.

The first thing you must consider before installing tile is the substrate – the surface you will lay your tile over. It is very important that the substrate be rigid, flat, and sound. If there is any flex in the substrate, your tile and grout will pop off the first time pressure is placed on the tile surface. There are three substrates, which usually come in sheets of 32" x 60", that are recommended for tile installation.

Cement backerboard – Cement backerboard is made of a cement-like material that is sandwiched between layers of fiberglass mesh. It is an excellent choice as a substrate in areas exposed to water.

Greenboard – This is a drywall-like product that is treated to resist moisture. It may be pale blue or green and is moisture-resistant but should

not be considered waterproof. It should be used in areas where contact with water is minimal.

Exterior plywood – Plywood, 1/2" to 3/4" is versatile and works well in low moisture areas.

Grout is another important element in tile installation. Grout has numerous functions ranging from keeping moisture from penetrating your substrate to adding dimension and beauty to your installation. The space between the tile is called the grout joint, and in relationship to handmade tile has a direct effect on which grout you choose for installation. Because handmade tile has irregular edges, the grout joint must be wider to accommodate the variations. Wider grout joints need to be filled with sanded grout, which is readily available at local hardware stores. It comes in powder form and must be mixed with liquid. Remember that even after the grout has been applied, it is not waterproof and must be sealed with a water-based sealer once or twice a year. You may also add latex or acrylic additives to the grout, which will not only give it more flexibility but will help with mildew and stain resistance.

Choosing your adhesive will depend on your installation site.

Mastic – Mastic is an inexpensive ready-mixed product that has great sticking power and is ideal for applying wall tile without the worry of the tile sliding down. Mastic should not be used for floors because it is not flexible, and cannot be leveled properly.

Thin-set mortar – Thin-set usually comes in powder form and is mixed with liquid according to the manufacturer's directions. It does not have immediate sticking power, which makes it a poor choice for walls. This adhesive forms a very strong and moisture-resistant bond. It is ideal for floors and can be leveled. It is important to add a latex additive because thin-set is very brittle and the latex will allow flexibility.

Here is a list of installation tools and a brief explanation of their uses. Your installation will determine which tools suit your needs. All the listed tools are available at local home improvement stores. Again, research your installation needs before you invest in any tools or materials. Because of the variety of installation possibilities, you might need specialized materials that are not listed to complete your job.

Before you begin, the first item on your list should be safety goggles and they should be worn during the entire installation process.

Snap cutter – A device that scores the tile like a glass cutter. After the scoring, pressure is applied to snap the tile along the scored line. This is ideal for straight cuts, but sometimes difficult to use on thicker handmade tile.

Nibbling tool – A plier-like tool used to nip rough cuts in a tile.

Wet saw – A saw that is used with water. As the blade turns, cutting through the tile, water is pumped onto the cutting site to cool the friction between the blade and the tile. Although this tool is an investment, it can be rented at local rental stores, and is an ideal tool for cutting tile. Familiarity with power tools will make operating a wet saw much easier.

Level – A level is a common tool with a floating bubble that is used to test horizontal and vertical surfaces for level and plumb.

Trowel – A notched tool used to apply mastic to the substrate. Your container of mastic will specify the notch size needed for applying the mastic according to your job specifications.

Spacers – Small plastic pieces used between tiles to space grout joints. You may or may not want to use spacers. Because handmade tile is so irregular, it might be a good idea to judge your grout lines by visually checking them rather than using spacers.

Grout float – A grout float works like a squeegee by pushing the grout into the joints.

Large sponge – Wipe the tile surface with a sponge to remove excess grout.

Chapter 10

Advice from the
EXPERTS

The Moravian Pottery and Tile Works.

Photo by Joe Jacobs.

Shrinkage

by Eric Rattan

Eric Rattan has been working with ceramics for over 20 years. His work has been sold nationally to both private and public collectors. Rattan recently received the Tile Heritage Foundation 2001-02 award, where his work was displayed in the Art Museum of the Americas in Washington, D.C.

A handmade tile from "scratch" begins with moist clay that loses all of its moisture content and therefore shrinks. It shrinks some in the first, or bisque, firing and shrinks more in the final firing. If you are aiming for a specific finished size, you need to start with a template that is larger than that size.

For the purpose of calculating shrinkage in a modular tile, such as a 4" by 4" tile, you would use "shrink rulers," pictured on page 95. These rulers show the inches already expanded by different percentages.

The clay catalog supplied by the manufacturer often lists the percentage of shrinkage you can expect from a clay body fired to its maximum temperature. If it is not listed in the catalog, call the manufacturer and ask. If the reply is 10%, simply turn to the 10% shrink ruler and make a 4" by 4" tile template using the shrink ruler as your guide. This ruler has the "inches" already expanded by 10% so that the fired tile will actually measure 4".

You can reduce the amount of shrinkage in a clay body by wedging in grog. Since the grog has already been fired, the more you add, the less clay will shrink. Remember, however, that grog can adversely affect texture and plasticity if too much is added.

Clay slip also shrinks radically. If you are brushing on slip to decorate a tile, trial and error will often determine a successful result. When slip is used to join pieces of clay in a relief tile, the mechanical bind can be strengthened by the use of vinegar. Mixing slip with half vinegar and half distilled water usually makes good "glue."

To control shrinkage in a freeform mosaic, you will likely have to trim the leather-hard clay to maintain even joints. Using similarly sized pieces minimizes your shrinkage problems if you choose this method of tile making. [*Author's note*: It is wise to execute geometric modular tiles if you are a beginner and save the freeform technique for later.]

Entire books have been written on glaze calculation and shrinkage. It isn't within the scope of this book to address all the variables. The beginning tile maker can achieve success by choosing a commercially prepared glaze designed to be fired at the same temperature as the clay body. Simply said, choose a cone 6 glaze for a cone 6 clay body.

The adventurous shrink tester should study the photo on page 94 of the oxide enhanced faux carpet. Shrinkage control is integral to the finished uninterrupted borders. This mosaic utilizes eight different clay bodies in four colors, each of which shrinks at a different rate. While creating this piece, I played a tape recording of my therapist's soothing voice which repeats, "It will work out…It will work out!"

Photo by Skot Weidemann.

Eric Rattan, "Autumn Color II," 1000 piece handmade floor tile faux carpet mosaic, 7' x 42".

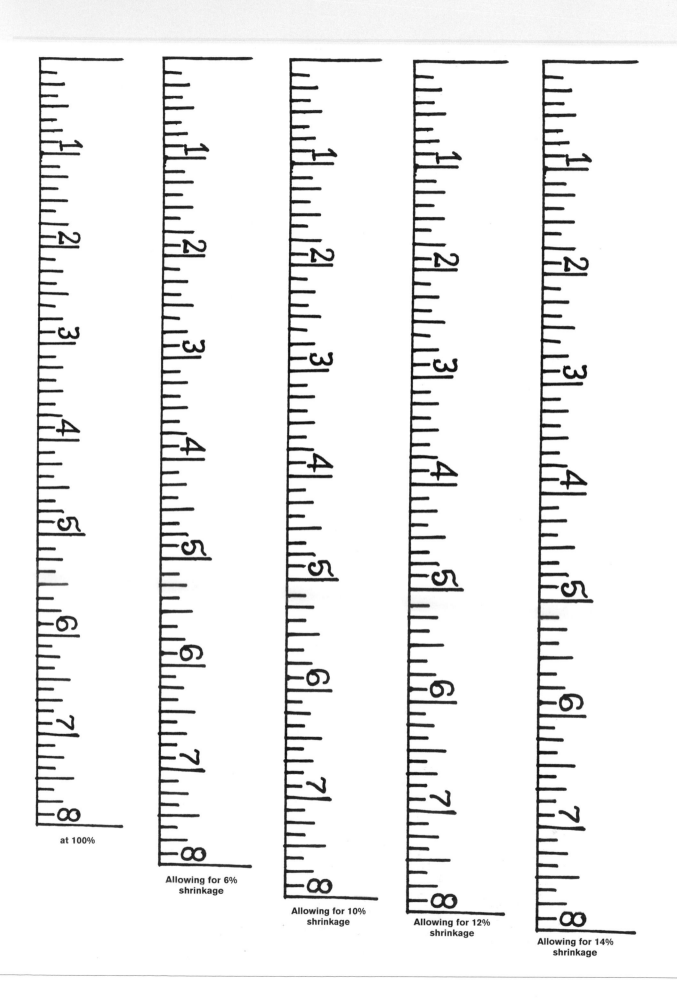

at 100%

Allowing for 6%
shrinkage

Allowing for 10%
shrinkage

Allowing for 12%
shrinkage

Allowing for 14%
shrinkage

Decorating with Handmade Tile

by Pamela Rosensweig

Pamela Rosensweig has 17 years of experience working with national tile companies. She has a degree in Buying and Merchandising from the Fashion Institute of Technology in New York City. Rosensweig currently designs the tile displays for the EXPO Design Center stores throughout the country.

With handmade tile, the more imperfections, the better the look. Each tile looks different, giving you the look of a beautiful piece of artwork.

Here are a few things to consider when designing with handmade tile: the expense of the tile and the installation, the overall look you are trying to achieve, the space where your tile will be installed, and the grout joints and color of grout.

Expense is usually the first thing people consider when they purchase an item. Handmade tiles are more expensive than machine-made tiles, so you need to consider your space and how to get the most for your money. Determine the square footage of your entire space (i.e., the length times the width), which should account for your field tile. Depending on what you are tiling, this can get very expensive. The difference in the amount of tile used in a fireplace installation and the amount needed for the bathroom will vary greatly. In a bathroom, you could tile just the tub surround or you could tile the bathroom wall halfway, three quarters, or from floor to ceiling. The square footage times the price per square foot will determine what will fit in your budget. Remember to allow for 10% overage for tile installed straight and 15% overage for any patterns. Even a good installer will need the extra tiles, which is considered a normal expense, and not having them may cost you more in the long run and could delay the installation.

If the price of the field tile is more than you can spend, you can lower the overall cost by using machine-made tile in combination with handmade tile. If you decide to go with handmade tile, consider what trim pieces will work. The linear footage and the size of the trim pieces will determine how many pieces you will need. Not all trim pieces come with finishing or turning corners. This is when a good installer becomes important. Corners must be mitered (cut at a 45% angle) to achieve a complete installation. Trim pieces can really add to a look by finishing where the tile ends and the directions change. Trim also adds to the overall texture.

Installation is a big consideration with handmade tile. It is more expensive to install handmade tile because cuts must be carefully considered. Machine-made tile takes less thought and planning and are so uniform that an installer can use spacers. Handmade tile must be laid out with an artist's eye. No spacers can be used, so it takes more time to install. Prices will vary, depending on demand and the expertise of the installer. If one installer's quote is much less than another's, this may not be the installer for you. Some installers may charge less if they are starting out because they may be experimenting on you. An installation by an inexperienced installer could lead to uneven grout joints or the installation could be so poor it could mean ripping out the tile, buying more, and having it installed a second time. Be careful of too good a deal.

Next, consider the overall space where the tile is being placed. Do you want to create focal points — areas the eyes are drawn to? Focal points in the kitchen could be behind the stove, the hood, or behind the sink. Or they could be all three of these areas. It depends on the look you want to achieve. Study decorating books and magazines to help determine what you prefer. In a bathroom, the focal point could be the tub surround, behind the tub, the shower wall, or around a mirror. A fireplace design should be completely drawn out by your designer ahead of time. The smaller the space, the more time you should

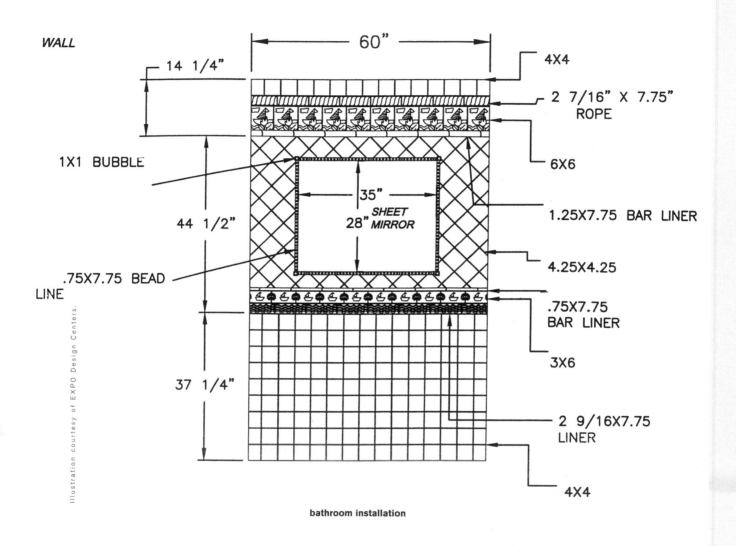

WALL

60"

14 1/4"

4X4

2 7/16" X 7.75" ROPE

1X1 BUBBLE

6X6

35"

28" *SHEET MIRROR*

1.25X7.75 BAR LINER

44 1/2"

4.25X4.25

.75X7.75 BEAD LINE

.75X7.75 BAR LINER

3X6

37 1/4"

2 9/16X7.75 LINER

4X4

bathroom installation

Illustration courtesy of EXPO Design Centers.

spend on planning to assure the biggest impact.

Color is another thing to consider. Color can be a very personal choice. If you've chosen tile and are nervous about the style or color, buy some samples and take them home with you. Leaving them in the room where they will be installed will help you make the final decision. If you plan to sell your house in the future, be very careful about color. If this is the case, neutrals are always safer to use. Paint and wallpaper can be replaced more easily than tile, although the right tile can help sell a house.

The more irregular your handmade tile, the wider the grout joint will have to be. A grout joint around 3/16" will work for most handmade tile. If the grout joints are any larger, they may crumble.

Cement can be used on larger grout joints, but it usually comes in gray. Gray blends with most color tiles and gives an old world look, which is very popular with handmade tile. You need to be wary of strong colored grouts, especially if they are being used with lighter colored tile. Some colors, such as black, can bleed into the tile, giving you a spidery veining around the edges of the tile. It is always safer to use a neutral grout that blends with the tile.

Always consider what is in the rest of the room. You must keep in mind the cabinets, fixtures, and appliances. Going to a one-stop store that carries everything from fixtures to cabinets makes working with your tile selection much easier.

Participating in Shows

by Diane Husson

Diane Husson is an award-winning Virginia-based artist whose work has been nationally published and internationally displayed. Her privately commissioned works are enjoyed by corporations and individuals throughout the United States.

So your first handmade tiles are a hit. Your mom and the neighbors like them. You get the feeling somewhere out there, buyers are waiting to get their hands on your tiles. One of the fastest ways to get your ceramic gems of creativity out there in front of people with open wallets is by participating in arts and crafts shows.

All arts and crafts shows are not created equal. They run the gamut in booth price, number of exhibitors, quality of arts/crafts, and the number of people who attend. Your first job is to find a show that will draw a crowd that will want to buy your work. If you have no prior experience with art shows, I recommend that you do some hands-on research. Target small shows in your area. Look in the paper and find out the dates. Next, talk a friend into visiting some of these shows with you. Seek out decorative clay exhibitors and ask them questions. I have found that artists are very open about the pros and cons of the shows they do. It is important that you talk to artists who are selling comparable artwork at comparable prices. A show could be a disaster for someone who paints large, expensive canvases, but great for you because your tiles are reasonably priced. While a competitor has work that is difficult to place, your work might make a good gift and fit any décor.

If you are visiting a show and it seems to have potential, find the show's organizers and get on their mailing list so you receive next year's application. While you're out scoping shows, take notes on the various displays. What do you like about the way various artisans show their wares? What turns you off? Keep these things in mind when you plan your own display. Remember that the way you interact with people is just as important as your artwork and your display. When you participate in art shows, you will be selling yourself as an artist. Be enthusiastic and above all, have fun.

Shows fall into many different categories. Here are some of the differences.

Outdoor arts and crafts shows. These shows are often run by some type of nonprofit or civic organization. Booth fees for outdoor (and indoor) shows vary greatly, based on the size, location, and prestige of the show. These shows are usually juried, meaning that artists who want to participate send in an application and several images (usually in slide form), along with a nonrefundable jury fee (usually between $15 and $25). The slides you send in will be viewed by one or more jurors. When they view slides, they may be given information about the process, size, and medium, without being given the artists' names. The jury commonly consists of artists from various media, gallery owners, or other "experts." Those who run the show give the jury the criteria to use to select artists.

Fine art and craft shows can be highly competitive, so it is in your best interest to hire a professional photographer to take your jury slides. Many shows now require a booth slide too. The jury will look at this slide to make sure you have a quality display and a cohesive body of work. They will also check to make sure you are actually selling what you say you'll be selling.

Festival shows. Art and craft shows are sometimes part of other festivals. Do your homework before you do a festival show. Festivals can draw tens or even hundreds of thousands of people, and the exposure can be excellent. They can be lucrative if you have the type of products and prices the crowd is looking for. However, if the main purpose of the festival is to drink beer and eat shellfish, then the artistic part of the event may take a backseat to the festivities.

To do an outdoor show you will need a tent. If you plan to do more than one outdoor art show per year, I recommend buying your own tent, based on quality and resistance to wind.

Diane Husson, "Garden of Joy."

Never buy a tent based on how inexpensive and easy to set up it is. When the first tropical storm blows through during the art show, you'll understand why. If you are not sure you want to do outdoor art shows and just want to get your feet wet, you can find the name of a tent rental company in the yellow pages.

Small craft bazaars. You will probably see lots of signs for craft shows and craft bazaars around Christmas time. They can be in church basements and elementary school gymnasiums, or art centers. Buying a table space is usually inexpensive. Sometimes these events are held in prosperous areas and can draw a reasonably affluent crowd. These types of shows are not usually juried, but photos or slides may be screened by the show directors to make sure you have crafted the items yourself and that they are of reasonable quality. If your tiles are well crafted and very affordable to the average person, gift-oriented craft shows can be a low risk way to try out the art/craft show realm. Display investment is usually minimal. You can sometimes get by with a fire retardant tablecloth, a cashbox, and a smile.

Large indoor craft shows. Some of these shows are run by professional promoters. Booth fees can be pricey. Many crafters gladly pay it because many of these shows, if well advertised, can draw 10,000 to 40,000 motivated shoppers who pay an admission charge to get in to see the artwork. Before signing a contract for a show, walk the show and ask a lot of questions. Scope out the types of the exhibitors and the crowds they draw. Talk to other clay artists if they are not busy with customers. If the show has the feeling of a flea market, or if you see too many country crafts, bunnies in dresses, fudge stands, and painted slate displays, run and don't look back. Those who attend these types of shows are probably not your market unless you plan to turn your handmade tiles into $5 trivets. Ask the show promoters what the "gate" attendance is and what their ad campaigns are. You want a show that is well advertised, established, and well attended.

Fine craft shows. Fine craft shows are usually held indoors and they are generally expensive to do. These shows are juried and some can be quite competitive. The degree of competition usually depends on the number of affluent shoppers and the amount of money they spend on the crafts. As a general rule, every artist wants to do the shows where a lot of money is changing hands. But you have to ante up. In addition to booth space costing hundreds of dollars, you will need to pay extra for electricity, a corner space, etc. Those who run the shows want your booth to look upscale. You'll need to provide your own professional display panels, a track lighting system, and carpeting. Doing indoor fine craft shows is a sizeable financial investment, and you may want to get further along on the learning curve before you jump in at this level.

Group shows, home shows, and open studios. Often several artists will band together and rent space or use someone's house or studio to run their own private show. These shows can be very effective if members of the group have a large mailing list, a good location, and time and money to sink into marketing the show. Open studios are events put on by a group of artists in the same geographic area. They decide on a date, publish and distribute directions to their studios, then sell their wares to the public. In the world of clay, these events can also be referred to as kiln openings.

Show Resources

Sunshine Artist magazine is a major national show and festival guide. It gives show listings, rates shows, and has helpful articles and insights pertaining to the world of art/craft shows. Throughout the magazine you will find the names of suppliers for tents, display panels, lighting systems, and more. (www.sunshineartist.com)

The Crafts Report is a trade publication dedicated to craft professionals, including artists and gallery owners. It lists various shows and contains ads for all types of suppliers of art/craft show equipment and services. The discussion group on their website (www.craftsreport.com) is a wonderful forum for learning about issues related to the business end of the craft world.

Artfair Sourcebook is an in-depth rating service covering the top art and craft shows in the country. Average sales, crowd size, contact names and phone numbers, and other vital information are provided in book form or via the Internet. This information is not cheap, but if you want to do shows seriously, it may be a good research tool for your library. (www.artfairsourcebook.com)

Photo by Anthony Verde.

Margie Hughto and Arts in Transit Staff, 81st Street Station MTA, Arts for Transit overview. Ceramic fabricator, Margie Hughto, mosaic fabricator, Miotto Mosaics.

Public Art

by Binnie B. Fry

Binnie Fry has been a ceramic tile dealer for the past 26 years, working on residential and commercial projects, with a particular interest in handmade tiles and mosaics. For the last two years, her work has concentrated on public art projects, and she assists artists who want to use tile in their projects by locating and selecting appropriate materials and providing technical specifications for the installation of the work.

When I speak of public art, I am referring to visual works of art created for specific public locations and available to public and often diverse audiences. Public artworks may be com-

missioned by agencies, private corporations, or individuals. Some are mandated by legislation, which requires the allocation of funds. Often a percentage of the cost of a construction project is allocated to integrate artwork into the overall project design. Others are generated by citizen groups who wish to enhance or revitalize a specific community or blighted community site. Sometimes an individual artist may have an idea for a project on public space, and successfully raise funds, both public and private, to create it.

Public art projects can be found throughout the country in dense urban areas as well as smaller towns or neighborhoods. The scope and size of projects may vary based on climatic conditions, regional stylistic considerations, and differences in state and local funding, but opportunities to find public settings for visual art are everywhere.

These settings include walls, walkways, parks, tunnels, and roadways. Many urban cen-

Photo courtesy of Joan Gardiner.

Joan Gardiner, Waterford Elementary School installation detail.

ters, among them Cleveland, Detroit, New York City, and Washington, D.C., have well-developed programs to enhance the use of public transportation by adding art to their rail stations, platforms, overpasses, garages, and bus stations. Many airports include public art. Smaller towns, as well as culturally distinct or affluent communities, find public art a successful way, on main streets and in town plazas, to establish a cohesive identity, a thoughtful view of history, or a sense of place, purpose, renewal, and promise.

Ceramic art has been a major category of public art projects nationwide, and includes painted murals, mosaic constructions, and dimensional tile construction. Some funding entities prefer flat mosaic or commercial tile works, but many are open to incorporating flat handmade tile as well as handmade relief tile in their projects. Some murals now gracing major walls consist entirely of handmade tiles. Others include handmade tiles as ornament, accent, or part of mixed-media construction. Examples of multimedia materials also featured are benches, archways, entryways, fountains, and signage.

The success of a public installation of ceramic handmade tiles depends not only on the way it physically and emotionally engages its audience, but also on the manner in which it is constructed. It is the challenge of every artist working on a tile project to be technically adept in building the project so that it is structurally sound and appropriate for its climatic or physical environment. Will the clay used be suitable if it is subject to freezing conditions? Will it be installed to prevent damage or delamination if subjected to vibration? Can it withstand foot traffic? What will happen if it is continually or seasonally under water?

Artists applying for public art commissions and opportunities will need to make themselves aware of and do careful research on local conditions and select or create their materials accordingly. As time has shown some early outdoor ceramic installations to be vulnerable to weathering and wear, artists should now expect to be asked to provide evidence that their materials and methods of installations are, indeed, suitable for a particular site. They may also be asked to provide guidelines for long range maintenance of their projects. Tile makers can avail themselves of con-

sultants or technical support staff from materials suppliers to facilitate these selections and recommendations. Some public art programs provide the services of architects and engineers to assist, and some provide experienced local installers who work regularly for that program.

Following are examples of recently completed public art projects using handmade tiles. Not all of the artists live in the communities where their work is installed. While this may complicate projects in terms of fabrication, installation, and coordination with local construction crews, it also is an opportunity for previously unseen work to infuse a community with a new artistic vision.

In Waterford, Virginia, tile artist Joan Gardiner, serving as Artist-in-Residence in an elementary school designated a National Landmark, submitted a proposal to complete an indoor mural measuring approximately six feet by 18 feet. The mural depicts Waterford at three stages of its history, the last being the present. Many public art projects are funded because they include the participation of local community members, particularly children and teens. The project then becomes a joint venture, and the final design may not emerge until the project is well underway.

For the "Millennium Wall," Gardiner designed and fabricated in her nearby studio, three small mural panels of 24 handmade illustrated 6" by 6" tiles, all essentially flat. She then worked in the school, exploring with the students the history of their community, as well as the history and uses of clay. With the help of their parents, she taught them to make the remaining dimensional tiles that surround her murals.

The children selected objects and tools relevant to the mural content and built their relief tiles from red clay slabs and clay bits. They used a series of techniques such as scoring, slip joining, and misting to build the images. They were taught to make molds to create multiple high relief border ties, and they used simple alphabet noodles to create quotations on the mural. A challenge specific to this project was the glazing, as not all glazes are approved for use by children.

In Landover, Maryland, multimedia public artist Jerome Meadows of Washington, D.C., and Savannah, Georgia, was funded by the Maryland

Jerome Meadows, Landover Metro, "I'm not afraid of tomorrow because I've seen yesterday and yesterday is beautiful." Quote by Janet Harmon Waterford.

State Department of Transportation Mass Transit Administration, through the Prince George's County Department of Public Works and Transportation, to create an artistic link for riders between the Metro they use and the community in which they live. Meadows is highly respected for his ability to capture the heart of a community. While this project can be considered "participatory," local input came from a dialogue with the community and community meetings rather than hands-on work. All of the tile was made by Meadows and his own staff at his Meadowlark Studios in Georgia and installed by his own crew in Maryland.

In this project, handmade tiles were only one element of a comprehensive plan composed of colored and raked concrete sidewalks and landscaping, into which the tiles were set. Fifty-nine panels composed of a total of 354 individual tiles were created. These arched units, measuring between 30" to 48" across, were formed of 1/2" light-colored stoneware clay, chosen for its ability to withstand traffic and freeze/thaw climates. Carved into the tiles were quotations and images relevant to the life of the local citizens, their history and concerns. One reads, "You must grow where you are planted," another, "Education is our passport to the future."

Glaze was applied by spraying, but the incised letters were hand glazed following application of a protective latex resist. Meadows is also in charge of the upcoming second phase of the project, which will involve structural work as well as landscaping.

One of the largest projects to date of tile maker Shel Neymark of Embudo, New Mexico, glorifies a very small and isolated town in southeast New Mexico. Having seen Neymark's earlier work in Albuquerque, community leaders of Artesia, a town rich in oil resources but in need of a facelift, asked Neymark to develop a tile design for the town's center, which had been ailing since fire destruction years before.

Neymark's Artesia Heritage Walkway is an excellent example of New Mexico's Main Street Revitalization Program, which promotes the efforts of privately funded nonprofit associations working to restore worn down public main areas. Funding was provided locally through Artesia's own nonprofit revitalization group. Fortunate in having a good budget, extensive freedom to be creative in his work, architectural and landscape assistance, and engineering help in developing the fountain structures, Neymark's only real problem in the 18-month-long project may have been the beginning of frost before final completion.

The Walkway is composed of several hundred square feet of handmade tiles made of frost-free clay refined by Neymark over his many years of outdoor work. It includes a pictorial tile archway over tile columns, five large tiled fountains, and below, an interconnecting tile stream. All tile work was done by Neymark and his assistants, but the sculptural underlying forms and the finished tiles were installed with the help of local contractors and community volunteers.

Weather conditions are uncertain in many areas where outdoor projects are under consid-

Shel Neymark, Heritage Park, walkway fountain, Artesia, New Mexico.

Judith Inglese, ceramic frieze for DART station, Dallas, Texas.

eration, and unexpected frosts can occur. The Dallas Area Rapid Transit Authority (DART) selected Judith Inglese of Amherst, Massachusetts, in a public competition, to create a large five feet by 140 feet frieze at the Tyler-Vernon Light Rail Station in just such an area. Inglese was selected based on her experience in erecting large outdoor murals in many different areas of the country with uneven climates.

Inglese's earlier murals often told important stories about the evolution of the area. This newer project did as well, conveying what she learned about the roots of the multiracial and ethnic community in which her mural would be installed. Inglese used clays formulated with grog added for outdoor safety, often leaving the faces of her subjects unglazed in red, brown, and gray natural clays. Recently, her signature style of cutting and piecing flat slabs to form her images has evolved to include more relief construction. All of the tiles built in Inglese's studio were marked and detailed on cartons, then transported to Texas and reassembled on site with local help.

Many projects involve other materials, such as metal and concrete, as hidden elements of their construction, but some tile artists incorporate these materials as very visible and deliberate elements of a design. Donna Billick did just that in "Families First," a 2 feet by 14 feet by 10 feet outdoor arched portal composed of precast concrete, commercial tile, topped with symbolic abstracted painted steel forms.

Billick, of Davis, California, is known for her terrazzo public works as well as tiled murals and mosaic sculptures. She is comfortable working on a large or small scale. The success of many of her projects results from well established relationships she has developed with fabricators in different trades who can assist in implementing her concepts.

Often, when tile artists prove the capacity to complete a complex competitive public project effectively, other opportunities arise in the same network to do new and different work. In New York City, tile artist Margie Hughto of Syracuse has worked on two very different projects funded by the Metropolitan Transportation Authority's

Donna Billick, "Families First," Sacramento, California.

Margie Hughto, Cortland Street Station, MTA, New York City.

Arts in Transit Program. Hughto was first selected by a competitive panel to work on the Cortland Street Station in downtown Manhattan's business district. Researching the rich history of New York's seaport, as well as its financial markets, Hughto designed and created hundreds of handmade relief tiles, incorporating designs symbolic of these two themes and using her layered glaze technique, that now cover the walls on multiple panels in her major solo work "Trade, Treasure, and Travel" completed in 1997.

Not all public artwork, including that done in ceramic, is permanent. Sometimes work is done with the clear knowledge that it is temporary because buildings and neighborhoods change, along with unexpected circumstances. What is enduring, however, is the public art movement, and the vitality that has been infused into bland, ordinary buildings, deteriorated areas, and vacant spaces by artistic vision. Makers of handmade tile have been a part of that. It is both a proud achievement and an open future.

Melody Ellis, "A Walk," terracotta and cement, cone 05, 15" x 20" x 2", 1999.

Mosaic and Decorative Techniques

by Melody Ellis

Melody Ellis received her initial education in tile work from the Tyler School of Art in Philadelphia. Ellis has had the benefit of working with some of the most talented tile artists in the country, including working at the Moravian Tile and Pottery. Her broad range of experience and expertise is mirrored in her work, which is exhibited throughout the country.

I am a ceramic artist who creates individual tiles as well as tile mosaics. I have learned and used two different methods of setting tile mosaics and have incorporated some of my own ideas with these to come to my current process.

A good way to start a mosaic is by creating a drawing on paper the same size as the finished mosaic. This allows for changes or corrections. Trace the final drawing onto heavy plastic sheeting with a permanent marker that can be erased and reworked on the plastic. This is a good time to determine how your image can be cut into manageable pieces. I generally keep my pieces between 1" and 6" in any direction. You can cut the image into a simple grid of square tiles, but a "jigsaw puzzle" method exploits the mosaic technique and incorporates grout as a linear visual element rather than trying to hide it. In this way, the grout lines become part of the design rather than a disruption of it. It isn't necessary to cut all the tiny pieces apart. If you keep your drawn lines a consistent width, when the mosaic is grouted, these will all appear to be individual pieces.

The plastic sheeting or original paper drawing is a great way to keep track of or re-create designs and gives you a place to jot measurements or glazing notations. It is also an important map should a piece break or warp and need to be remade. You can also write numbers on the plastic to correspond with numbers written on the backs of tiles. It is amazing how confusing all those pieces can be after firing.

Spray a leather-hard slab with water and lay the plastic drawing on top, smoothing it on firmly with a rubber tip. A sharp pencil is the best tool to trace the design onto the clay. Be sure to retrace these lines after removing the plastic. They must be deep enough to hold grout, and of an even width so that actual cuts and uncut lines all appear the same (that is, when filled with grout, all will appear to be cut apart whether they are or not). In this way, you can create the appearance of an intricately set mosaic without having to fuss over hundreds of soft tiny bits.

After adding any desired detail, cut the pieces apart at the predetermined lines, and bevel or undercut the bottom edges so the mosaic pieces fit together snugly on the surface. More detail work can be done after cutting the pieces apart. The mosaic will be mounted on plywood, so the edge pieces can be fit in an L-shape with side extensions, or individual side tiles can be created if you want to cover the sides of the plywood. Alternatively, the exposed sides of the plywood can be painted after grouting.

After glazing and firing, lay out the mosaic in its final form with about 1/8" between each piece. If the complete mosaic is a square or rectangle, check it with a square.

In my own work I have embraced grout as a visual element beyond common usage. I use both flat lined drawings and carved relief in my designs, and try to incorporate details that will catch and hold the grout for greater definition. When carving a relief area, I often outline the shape with a deep line to keep the grout from wiping away. This ensures that the form will stand out as a linear design as well as a relief form.

My tile designs are made using Longhorn red earthenware. They are generally either lined drawings colored with slips and underglazes or bare clay with relief carving. I once-fire to cone 05 and grout for a simple but dramatic result. I use the same methods and materials with my mosaic work, but often use both flat and carved areas in a single piece, and glazes in addition to slips. I always finish by sealing the clay with linseed or cooking oil. This simple approach to surface allows the work to be gently cleaned with dish soap and water and re-oiled as needed.

I find a great deal of enjoyment in creating tile mosaics and the most exciting part comes in grouting, when the whole piece is pulled together and finally revealed. The process outlined above will provide a fairly simple guide to creating your own mosaic, with rewarding results.

Chapter 11

PROJECTS

There are many uses for handmade tiles beyond the typical backsplash and floor covering. The following projects will not only expand your idea of where you can use your tiles, they will demonstrate different techniques that were used to create them.

Culinary Tiles

The bases of this project are simple 4" by 4" tiles. The variations in the project revolve around which decorative treatment you choose, and how you form the fork or spoon.

You will need:
- clay
- fork and spoon template
- four 4" x 4" tiles, bisque fired
- gloss glaze – clear, cobalt blue
- underglaze – red, light pink or peach, green, brown
- overglaze – metallic
- stylus
- potter's tool
- pencil
- ruler
- small brush
- mop brush
- air gun
- 4" paper doily

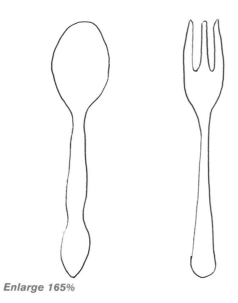

Enlarge 165%

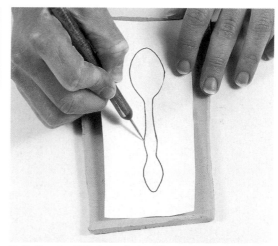

1. Roll out a ¼" slab of clay. Trace the spoon and fork patterns on paper. Place the paper template on the slab of clay and use a stylus to trace over the design. Make two spoons and two forks.

2. Peel back the pattern to make sure the design is transferred to the clay.

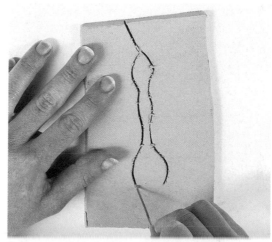

3. Use a potter's tool to cut out the design.

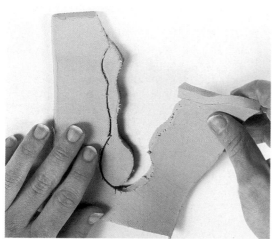

4. Carefully peel away the excess, and allow the clay to firm up.

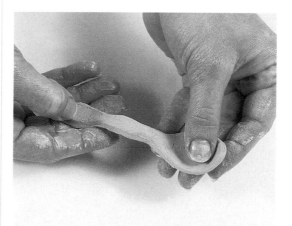

5. After the clay is firm enough to handle, model the design into a more realistic shape. Using a real spoon or fork as a guide helps. Set the designs aside until completely dry, then bisque fire to the recommended temperature. Once they are bisqued, you can easily handle the pieces for decoration.

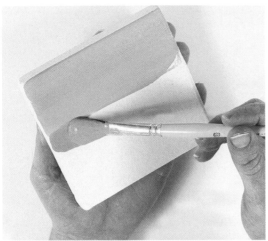

6. Tile #1 was achieved by glazing the entire surface in a solid color, in this case a glossy cobalt blue.

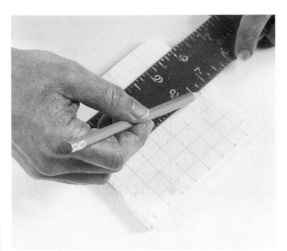

7. Tile #2 has a red and white checkered pattern done in underglaze. With a pencil, mark off the checkered pattern and lightly draw the pattern on the bisque tile.

8. With a small brush, paint every other square with underglaze. With a mop brush apply a clear glaze over the entire surface, being careful not to smear the underglaze.

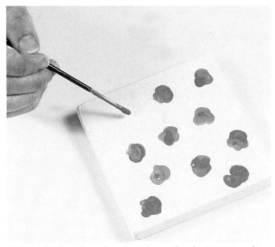

9. Tile #3 has hand-painted rosebuds scattered across the surface. Use red underglaze to paint rough circles for the rosebuds.

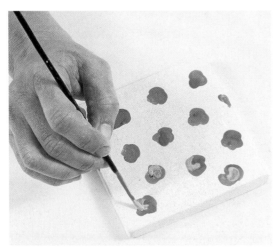

10. With the same brush, brush light pink or peach underglaze commas over the center of each rose. The more the colors blend, the more depth you can achieve in the center of each rose.

11. Paint on the leaves with green underglaze using the same comma motion. Using a mop brush, glaze over the entire surface with a clear gloss glaze.

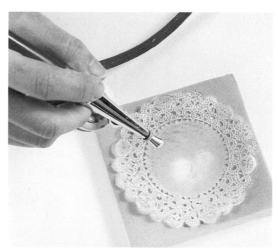

12. Tile #4 was created by placing a 4" paper doily over a bisque field tile as a stencil. Thin some brown underglaze with water and use an air gun to spray the glaze over the doily and tile.

13. Let the underglaze dry a moment before peeling off the doily. With a mop brush, apply clear gloss over the entire surface.

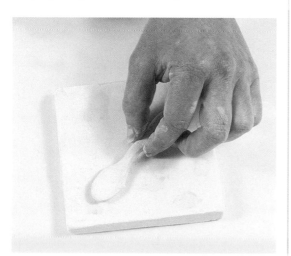

14. Once the base tiles are completed and gloss glazed, completely dip the spoons and forks in clear glaze and position them on the glazed field tiles. Place the tiles in the kiln and fire to maturity. The tile and the clay design pieces will fuse together in the kiln once the glaze starts to melt. After the pieces are fired, paint the cutlery with a metallic overglaze and fire a third time according to the manufacturer's instructions.

Twig Tiles

Twig tiles are easy and fun to do. The same principle used to create the twig tile can be used to create other tiles. By substituting other items found in nature like pinecones, leaves, or acorns, you can create an unlimited array of tiles without having to sculpt a thing.

The twig tile has many uses, from the picture frame shown, to a tile border.

The 4" by 4" pinecone tile was cast using the same method as the twig. Because the pinecone is so round, half of it was cut off before placing it on a blank field tile.

You will need:
- wood picture frame
- clay
- potter's needle
- plaster mold (see page 42)
- sharp scraping tool
- ceramic cement

1. The best twig or branch for this project is one that is straight, but with a little character such as small knots along the edges. The bark should be smooth and the twig cleanly cut on the edges. Measure the picture frame and cut twigs to match the length of the sides and top and bottom. Or, you can use twigs slightly longer so they will over-hang the frame.

2. The most important part of this project is the prep work for casting the twig. Roll out a clay slab approximately ⅛" thick. This slab will be the base of the tile. Lay the twig on top of the slab and trace its contours with a potter's needle, cutting out the twig shape.

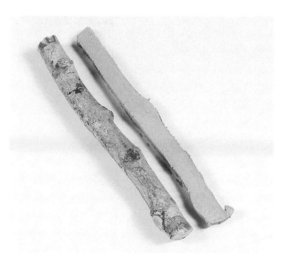

3. With the twig and slab side by side, you can see that they have the same silhouette.

4. Press the twig onto the slab, which now becomes the base of the tile.

5. Fill in the undercut area that runs between the base and the underside of the twig. Make small coils of clay and use them to fill in the gap. It is important to make sure there are no undercuts before you cast the twig. If there are, the plaster will run behind the undercut and it will be almost impossible to remove the twig from the mold.

Refer to page 42 for instructions on how to make a plaster mold of the twig. Don't apply mold release on the twig because that will ruin the absorptive properties of the plaster. Because the twig is wood and will swell after soaking up the moisture from the plaster, it usually takes a bit of work to remove the twig from the mold.

6. After the twig is removed from the mold, use a sharp tool to scrape out any bark left in the mold. The second casting is likely to be better than the first. Press clay in the first twig mold, then recast it. This will give you a clean mold because you are casting clay, and it will allow you to add any texture if the first twig was lacking.

The twig picture frame was easily constructed by using a plain wood picture frame as its base. It is best to use ceramic cement to attach the clay twigs because a glue gun does not have the strength to hold the tile. Remove the glass from the frame and cement the twigs directly on the wood picture frame.

This tile layout is an example of how the twig tile can be utilized as a border within a tile installation. The green 2" by 2" tiles are made by casting small leaves.

House Numbers

The house numbers use the sprigging technique that is explained on page 74. The numbers could have been placed on one large tile and made into one unit, but having each number on a separate tile showcases each one on its own. Each tile was stamped with a different pattern, but used the same color and technique to unify them. After completion, they can either be cemented into place or installed as you would any other tile. If they are going outside, make sure the clay body has been fired to maturity. This will insure as little water absorption as possible.

You will need:
- four 4" x 4" moist clay tiles
- stylus
- potter's tool
- mop brush
- small brush
- various rubber stamps (the design should be deep enough to leave an impression)
- cobalt blue underglaze
- clear gloss glaze
- slip

1. Roll out a ¼" slab of clay. Use the templates on page 120 to trace the desired numbers on paper. Use a photocopier to reduce or enlarge the numbers as needed. Place the paper templates on the slab of clay and use a stylus to trace over the numbers. Peel back the pattern to make sure the designs are transferred to the clay. Use a potter's tool to cut out the numbers. Carefully peel away the excess and allow the clay designs to firm up.

2. While the numbers are firming up, stamp designs into the unfired field tiles. The tiles shown were stamped with a random pattern using commercial stamps. You can stamp with anything that leaves a pattern and gives some texture.

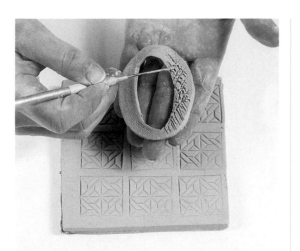

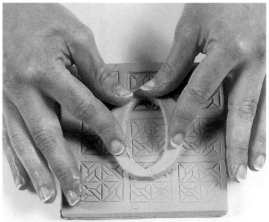

3. Lay the numbers on your tile to get a general position and use a potter's tool to gently score the backs of the clay numbers and the tile with a hatching pattern. Add a bit of slip to both the numbers and the tile to create a strong bond between the two.

4. Firmly place the clay numbers in the middle of the stamped field tiles.

Allow the tiles to dry completely, then bisque fire according to the clay's bisquing temperature.

Decorating the bisque tiles is a two-part process. For this project I used cobalt blue underglaze for both the background tiles and the numbers.

5. Mix a small quantity of underglaze with water to create a wash.

6. With a mop brush, brush the wash over the background tiles, allowing it to accumulate in the stamped detail.

7. Use a small brush to apply two to three coats of undiluted underglaze to the clay numbers. Complete the project by brushing the entire surface with a clear gloss glaze and fire accordingly.

Mirror

You will need:
- mirror with frame
- clay
- rolling pin
- four 4" by 4" field tiles for corners
- six 4" by 8" field tiles for center pieces
- plaster mold (see page 42)
- ceramic cement
- potter's needle
- paintbrush
- carving tool
- loop tool

Like the twig project, this project uses a traditional tile in a nontraditional way. Making this mirror will teach you lessons that are important for tile making. The first lesson involves the corner pieces of the mirror. You will notice that the pattern works itself around the corner of the mirror without interruption. But did you notice that because the mirror's top and bottom are symmetrical, there are actually two different corners? One corner scrolls left and the other corner scrolls right. There are actually three different pieces in this mirror – two corners and one large center piece. This idea becomes important when you are creating tile borders for other applications.

If you are doing a fireplace, you will need to turn the corner of the firebox without interrupting the pattern flow. To do this, you will have to design a corner piece.

The second lesson involves your ideas about where tile can be applied. This is a freestanding mirror but the tile could have been applied directly to a wall around a hanging mirror. Because the corner tiles are 4" by 8", they are large enough to go around a fireplace. Or these tiles could be used to create a border along a stove backsplash or tub surround.

These tiles are developed by layering clay. The tiles aren't sprigged and the clay isn't fired, only cast in plaster.

Template #1 – center

1. *Roll out a ¼" clay slab. Trace the three templates on paper. Use a photocopier to enlarge or reduce the templates to fit your mirror. Transfer the templates to the clay slab and cut out the designs with a potter's needle.*

Template #2 – right corner

Template #3 – left corner

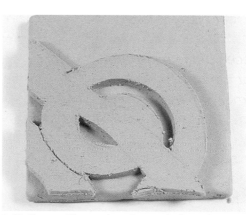

2. *Pull away the excess clay and place the cutout designs directly on blank field tiles. Because these tiles will be cast, they do not need to be scored or bonded with slip. Layering the designs allows you to have a clean background. If you were carving directly into the clay to get this relief, you would have to work hard to get the background free of tool marks.*

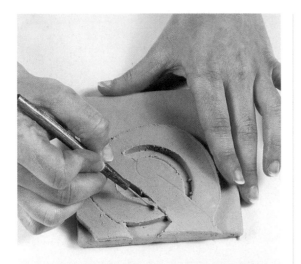

3. Use a sharp carving tool, such as a finger tool, to carve out the designs where they pass each other. The illusion of one piece passing under the other is achieved by allowing one piece to appear higher. In the photo, you can see how the ribbon appears to pass under the other ribbon. Carving down into the design and allowing one layer to appear higher gives the appearance that the other ribbon is going under it.

4. Use a sharp loop tool to create the incised lines. The loop tool pulls out the excess clay, giving you a ribbed look.

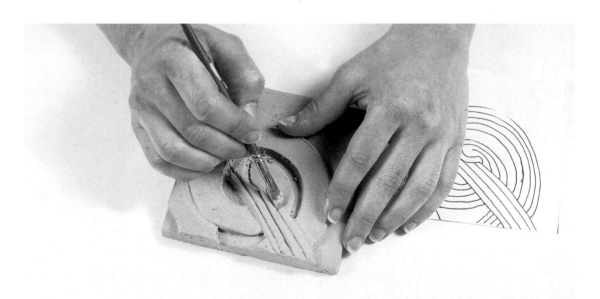

5. Clean up the tiles with a paintbrush. Paintbrushes are wonderful carving tools for clay. This brush has short flat bristles strong enough to move the clay around. Clean up the tiles and wipe any tool marks away. Also take notice of any undercuts and eliminate them.

6. Refer to page 42 for instructions on making a plaster mold. Make one plaster mold for the right corner, one for the left corner, and one for the center piece. For this mirror, I cast two clay right corners, two left corners, and six center pieces using the plaster molds.

7. Remove the clay castings from the plaster and allow them to dry completely.

8. After each piece is completely dry, bisque fire.

9. These tiles were glazed with a matt celadon blue glaze and fired to the glaze's listed temperature.

10. Attach the tiles to your frame using a ceramic adhesive or mastic, then grout the joints between each tile.

Chapter 12

The GALLERY

Diane Husson, "To Heal the Brokenhearted." White earthenware carved and cast in three parts, bisqued cone 04, glaze and underglaze fired at cone 06, gold luster and refired at cone 018.

Caren A. Goodrich, "Rabbit," 11" x 15¾", 2001.

Paul Lewing, "Fish Tub," china-painted tile, 18" high x 12" long, 2000.

Diane Husson, "Les Cadeux de la Mer" (Gifts from the Sea), carved stoneware, cone 6, 21" x 29". Carved from a slab. Underglaze applied to greenware and fired to cone 6. Additional underglazes and clear glaze applied, refired to cone 06.

Bob Jewett, "Woman in Blue."

Pat and Dave Dabbert, "Egret."

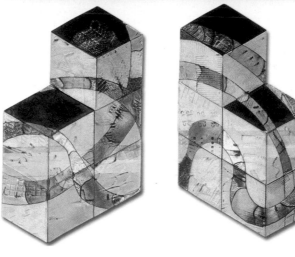

Phyliss Pacin, "Small Island City 5 & 6," wall sculpture, raku fired clay, 22" x 27" x 1", 1999.

Photo by Peter Smith.

Kim Gore, "Bacchus/Grape," fireplace surround.

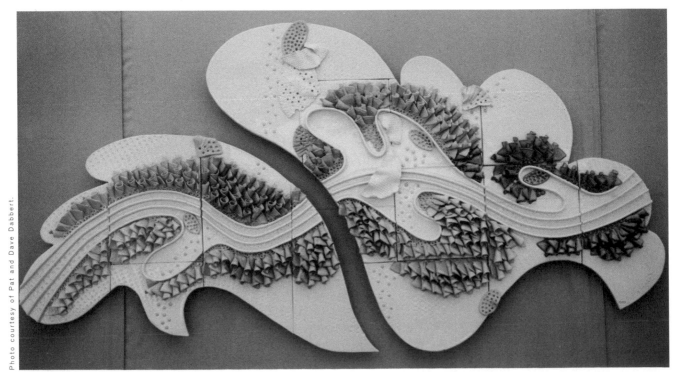

Photo courtesy of Pat and Dave Dabbert.

Pat and Dave Dabbert, "Coral Wave III."

Kim Gore, "Art Deco," fireplace surround with 20" x 20" figure tile.

Photo by Melody Ellis.

Melody Ellis, "Turnip Tile," earthenware with black grout detail, 2001.

Mary and Tim Pritchard, "Bear Scene," 1997. Hammond Bay Art Studio.

Jennifer Heynen, "Ceramic Border Table," handmade tiles and mosaics, 36" x 36" x 16" high.

Helen Helwig and Niki Glen, "Flora and Fauna of Arizona" detail.

Helen Helwig and Niki Glen, "Flora and Fauna of Arizona," amador clay, flagstone, river rock.

Helen Helwig and Niki Glen, "Butterfly Garden Bench," handmade clay pieces and commercial stone tile.

Francoise Choveau, "Planter," 12" x 8" x 4".

Gary Carlos, "Youth Voices" detail, directed by Gary Carlos and Ali Vieira.

Mary and Tim Pritchard, "Leaf Mosaic," 2001. Hammond Bay Art Studio.

About the Author

Kristin Peck currently lives in Virginia Beach, Virginia, with her husband David and their two sons. She has been involved in ceramics for the past eight years, motivated by what inspires most people – a love for creation. She started her own handmade tile company, Blackwater Tile Inc., which now distributes tile nationally through Home Depot's EXPO Design Centers. Through her company, she has designed tile featured on HGTV's "Dreamhouse." Kristin is also a contributor to national magazines like *Fine Homebuilding* and *Ceramic Industry*, on the subject of handmade tile. Spreading the art of handmade tile has been her goal through public speaking engagements with organizations like the National Kitchen and Bath Association and tile workshops around the country.

Artists and Contributors

Donna Billick
Billick Rock Art
35301 Rd. 31
Davis, CA 95616

Barbara Bloom
Bloom4@juno.com

Lisa Burt
Larkspur Art Tile
659 Weston Rd.
Larkspur, CO 80118

Gary Carlos
(619) 640-7932

Dennie Chiavarini
3843 Thaxton Ln.
Virginia Beach, VA
23452

Michael Cohen
Tiles by Michael
Cohen
107 Amherst Rd.
Pelham, MA 01002

Francoise Choveau
Rex Studio
rexstudio@hotmail.com

Mary Collier
5217 Quarry Ln.
Virginia Beach, VA
23464
maryarticraku4u@aol.
com

Pat and Dave Dabbert
Dabbert Studio
4819 Hoyer Dr.
Sarasota, FL 34241
(941) 925-9929

Melody Ellis
Lib_mee@shsu.edu

Epro Tile
156 E. Broadway
Westerville, OH
43081
(614) 882-6990

Binnie B. Fry
Specialty Tiles, LLC
1241 Titania Ln.
McLean, VA 22102
(703) 790-9018
binniefry@aol.com

Joan Gardiner
21103 Unison Rd.
Unison, VA 20117
(540) 554-8473

Yvonne George
George Designs
(407) 359-3211
redclay27@cs.com

Phyllis Gillispie
pgillispie@blackwater-
tile.com

Caren A. Goodrich
caren16@aol.com

Kim Gore
Hand Sculpted Tile
1527 Bauman Ave.
Royal Oak, MI 48073

Karen Hailey
(615) 661-9222
jhailey@home.com

Helen Helwig
Southwest Public Art
Group
Swpag4@aol.com

Diane Husson
www.newrelics.com
diane@newrelics.com

Jennifer Hynen
www.bloomington.in.
us/-handmade

Margie Hughto
6970 Henderson Rd.
Jamesville, NY 13078
(315) 469-3609

Judith Inglese
592 Main St.
Amherst, MA 01002
(413) 253-7658

Bob Jewett
Wilburton Pottery
P.O. Box 40161
Bellevue, WA 98015

Linda Leighton
Higher Fire Clay
Studio
2132 Regent St.
Madison, WI 53705

Paul Lewing
pjlewing@worldnet.att.
net

Scott Lykens
412 Long St.
Cambridge, OH
43725

Jerome Meadows
Meadowlark Studios
915 Waters Ave.
Savannah, GA 31404
(912) 233-7659

Shel Neymark
Architectural
Ceramics
P.O. Box 25
Embudo, NM 87531
(505) 579-4432

Phyllis Pacin
ppacin@yahoo.com

Kristin Peck
Blackwater Tile Inc.
dpeck@blackwater-
tile.com

Eric Rattan
Santa Fe Design
Studio
(608) 231-1884

Pamela Rosensweig
Pamela_rosensweig@
homedepot.com

Seneca Tiles
7100 S. Country
Rd. 23
Attica, OH 44807
(419) 426-3561

Bob Timberlake
(800) 992-2811
www.bobtimberlake.com

Linda Warner
picturemaker@media
one.net

Sue Werschkul
Illahe Tileworks
695 Mistletoe Rd. #F
Ashland, OR 97520

Helen Weisz
1775 Hillside Rd.
Southampton, PA
18966

Axner Potter Supply
(800) 843-7057
www.axner.com
Clay, glazes, full online catalog, equipment and supplies

Bailey Ceramic Supply
(800) 431-6067
www.baileypottery.com
info@baileypottery.com
Ceramic supplies, kilns, glazes, clay

Bennet Pottery
(800) 432-0074
Full line of equipment and supplies

Bisazza Mosaics
www.bisazzausa.com
Glass mosaics

Davens Ceramic Center
(770) 451-2105
Ceramic supplies, glass and glass frit

Florida Clay Art Co.
(800) 211-7713
Tile supplies, kilns, glazes

Georgies Ceramic & Clay Co.
(800) 999-2529
http://georgies.com
georgies@worldnet.att.net
Ceramic equipment, supplies, tile cutters

Great Lakes Clay and Supply
(800) 258-8796
www.greatclay.com
Ceramic supplies, equipment, clay, educational material

Mason Color Works, Inc.
(330) 385-4400
Mason stains, minimum purchase for wholesale price

Mid-South Ceramic Supply Co.
(615) 242-0300
www.opulenceglaze.com
Opulence glazes, full line of ceramic equipment, glazes, and supplies

North Star Equipment, Inc.
(800) 231-7896
Call for information, price list, dealers

Orton Ceramic Foundation
P.O. Box 2760
Westerville, OH 43086-2760
(614) 895-2663
www.ortonceramic.com
info@ortonceramic.com

Scutt Ceramic Products
(503) 774-6000
Call for a list of Scutt dealers

Tile Council of America, Inc.
100 Clemson Research Blvd.
Anderson, SC 29625
(864) 646-8453

Tile Heritage Foundation
P.O. Box 1850
Healdsburg, CA 95448
foundation@tileheritage.org
Magazine and quarterly newsletter

Index

More Instructional Books
From Krause Publications

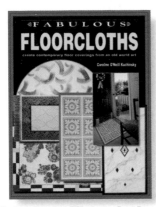

Fabulous Floorcloths
Create Contemporary Floor Coverings from an Old World Art
by Caroline O'Neill Kuchinsky

The first book dedicated to making canvas floorcloths. Contemporary or antique, a floorcloth transforms an ordinary floor into a work of art. The step-by-step instructions guide you through projects easily. Choose designs and color schemes in 14 projects divided into simple to advanced.

Softcover • 8¼ x 10⅞ • 128 pages
60 color photos • 225 color diagrams
FLODEC • $19.95

The Kiln Book
Materials, Specifications & Construction, Third Edition
by Frederick L. Olsen

Author Fred Olsen draws on over 40 years of experience to offer complete plans and instructions for building kilns of all sizes and purposes in this third edition of the definitive guide on kiln design and construction. Design highly efficient kilns using newly available refractory materials, updated designs and building methods for walls, arches and flues, and new safety equipment.

Hardcover • 8¾ x 11¼ • 288 pages
600 b&w photos & illustrations
16-page color section, 40 color photos
KILN3 • $44.95

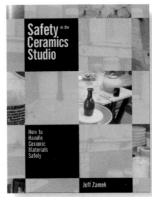

Safety in the Ceramics Studio
by Jeff Zamek

Use this comprehensive and detailed reference to stay safe in your ceramics studio. Your health and safety are the focus of this new book, which covers everything from ceramic toxicology to safe handling of raw materials, and provides guidelines for using clays, glazes, tools, kilns, and other equipment.

Softcover • 8½ x 11 • 160 pages
100 b&w photos • 16-page color section
SAFCM • $21.95

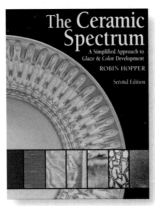

The Ceramic Spectrum
A Simplified Approach to Glaze & Color Development, Second Edition
by Robin Hopper

Author Robin Hopper brings 45 years of experience and education to his new edition of this ceramist's staple. With easy to follow and understand directions, accompanied by photos, charts and drawings, covering Egyptian pastes, high texture glazes and flux variation triaxial, among other topics, this is a must-have for any ceramist or potter.

Softcover • 8¼ x 10⅞ • 256 pages
300 color photos
CESP2 • $44.95

Arnold Grummer's Complete Guide to Paper Casting
by Arnold and Mabel Grummer

You'll learn everything you need to know about the craft of paper casting in this exciting new book. From the basic steps of making your own paper casts, to using everyday objects for making your own molds, authors Arnold and Mabel Grummer answer all of your questions. You'll find easy-to-follow instructions, detailed photographs, helpful tips, and ideas for embellishment. Includes 12 exciting projects for home décor and gift items such as plaques, baskets, and more!

Softcover • 8¼ x 10⅞
96 pages • 150 color photos
PCAST • $16.95

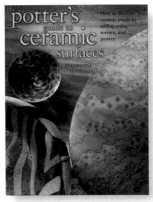

The Potter's Guide to Ceramic Surfaces
by Jo Connell

Learn how to make your ceramic pieces extraordinary works of unique art with this fascinating technique book. In this photo-intensive full-color text, you will find more than 70 techniques, such as post-firing, multiple firings and decorative processes used at the biscuit stage. Each includes detailed, step-by-step instructions to inspire you to add color, texture and pattern to your ceramic pieces.

Hardcover • 8½ x 11 • 160 pages
300+ color photos
ACMDE • $27.95

Shipping & Handling: $4.00 first book, $2.25 each additional. Non-US addresses $20.95 first book, $5.95 each additional.
Sales Tax: CA, IA, IL, NJ, PA, TN, VA, WI residents please add appropriate sales tax.
Satisfaction Guarantee: If for any reason you are not completely satisfied with your purchase, simply return it within 14 days of receipt and receive a full refund, less shipping charges.

To order, call 800-258-0929 Offer CRB2
M-F 7am-8 pm, and Sat 8am-2 pm.
www.krausebooks.com
Krause Publications, Offer CRB2, P.O. Box 5009, Iola WI 54945-5009